TAKE YOUR SH!T *to the* NEXT LEVEL

How to be the best version of yourself

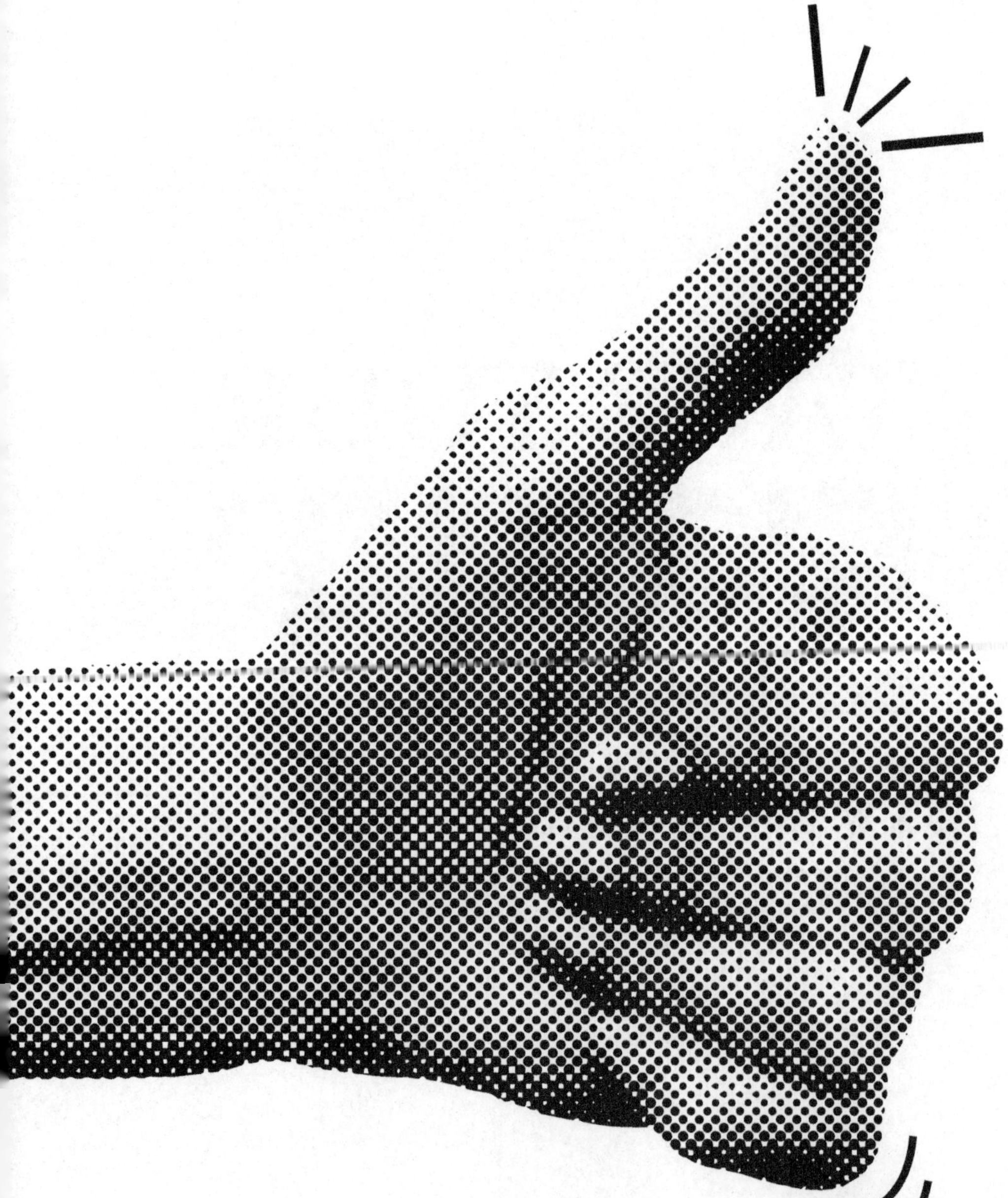

TAKE YOUR SH!T TO THE NEXT LEVEL

How to be the best version of yourself

Sian Winfield

ABOUT THE AUTHOR

Sian Winfield

ABOUT THE AUTHOR

Sian Winfield is a leading Entrepreneur Coach & Consultant who brings clarity, direction and dynamic growth to the people and businesses she works with.

Sian has spent the last two and a half decades working with those who have made the choice to take action. From the fitness industry as a fitness professional to NLP coach and trainer working with Traders to attain peak performance in London City. And after 15 years working in operations in start-ups, Sian started her own company within which she had the fortune of being involved with the successful growth and scaling of over 250 start-ups.

Alongside this Sian has empowered hundreds of entrepreneurs internationally through coaching individually and group programmes. Most recently Foundervine & Barclays Black Founder Accelerator Programme and mentoring for The Peter Jones Foundation. Also delivering workshops for the UK's most renowned Accelerator LMarks and their DPD EcoLabs and working with the Italian Trade Agency on their chosen start-ups to grow in the UK and world-wide.

This diverse experience forms the foundation of her approach, offering valuable insights into achieving success.

Sian Winfield

Cover and typesetting by Dave George
at GeorgeCreative.uk.

Printed and bound in the UK.

ISBN: 978-1-3999-8516-1

Dedicated to Soni.

The single best thing to ever happen.
Thank you for being my son,
friend and teacher.

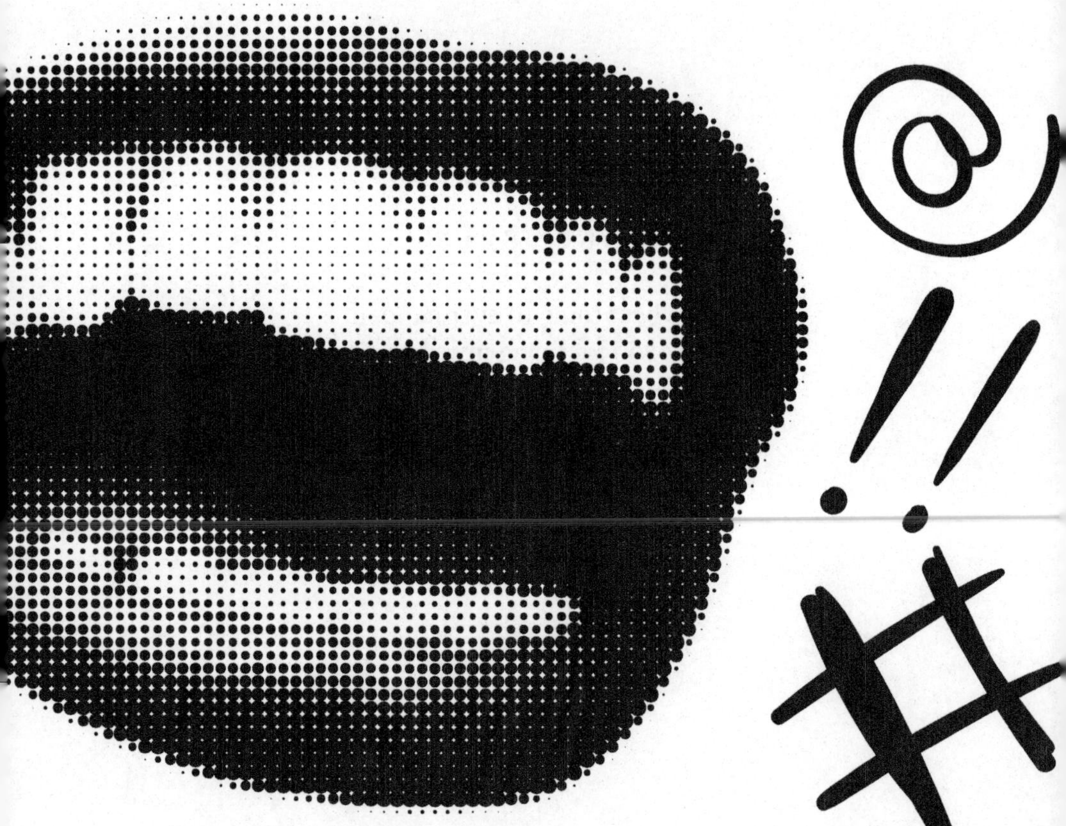

TAKE YOUR SH!T TO THE NEXT LEVEL

Sian Winfield

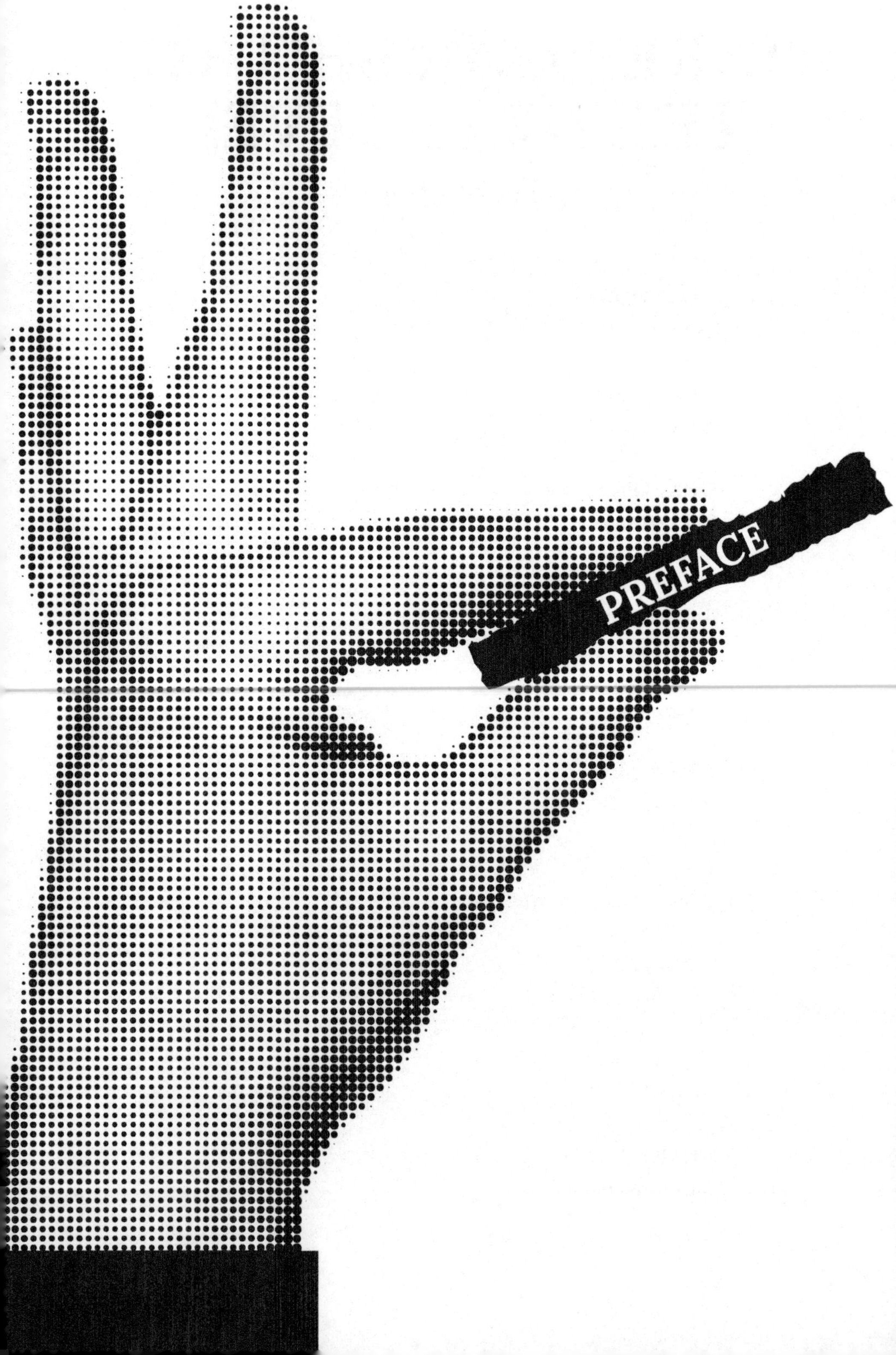
PREFACE

PREFACE

This preface I have written last and interestingly, having flown through writing this book to this point, now I am not sure where to start. I think I'm just going to close my eyes and pick a spot.

I really give a sh!t about other people's success.

Now this book isn't about me, it is about sharing learning on a wider platform to be able to impact as many people as possible. However, my younger years have played a large part in where my lessons, skills and attributes have developed over time.

Leaving home at a young age, I quickly figured out that if you are brave and just crack on regardless that you can pretty much get through anything. That anything is possible. Yes, it was tough and I'm not going to underplay that, however what has maintained my growth regardless is that I just took the actions that I needed to with constant movement forwards. Even when I didn't want to.

Admittedly, I became too independent for many years, however there is true power behind this to getting things done. The bravery and attributes I had to develop in my earlier years enabled me to drive for change for myself and others with real power. Bringing solid results and growth for the people and businesses that I work with, never mind what I have been able to achieve myself.

I kicked off my experience 25 years ago in the fitness industry where I was a successful PT (personal trainer) for clients in and around the Square Mile, lots of Traders and CEOs and Senior Executives. Fascinated by the fact that some people would train and others would struggle I further studied NLP, Neurolinguistic Programming and how it can be used to substantially elevate your game.

After applying these principles to my clients' training, I was asked to design a training course for a trading company inspired by a well-known book on NLP for Traders and Investors. Learning to trade and rolling this out fed my fascination with peak performance for sure.

PREFACE CONT...

The next 15 years I spent in operations helping start-ups to grow. With my strong ability to build a company and to read and motivate people, I soon found myself being headhunted for roles.

Today I wear many hats. Founder of CoStartup, which has successfully helped grow over 250 companies from multiple sectors and stages over the last 8 years, with a mission to relaunch as a start-up hub where we plan to share this learning on a wider scale. I coach and consult start-ups and scale-ups, entrepreneurs, and executives in business growth, from small start-ups right through to multi-million-pound companies.

I also contribute to Accelerator programmes such as Foundervine and Barclays Black Founder Accelerator programme and most recently with LMarks supporting DPD and their cohort. I mentor for great companies like 20/20 Levels and the Peter Jones Foundation, of Peter Jones, BBC Dragons Den. This diverse experience forms the foundation of my approach, offering valuable insights into achieving success.

From all this I've learnt that the opportunity for true success comes from your ability to use your time in the best possible way, taking smart consistent actions with the end goal in mind, while maintaining the best version of yourself at the core.

> ***You are the filter within which you see the world***, how you perform is the tool within which you ***get things done***.

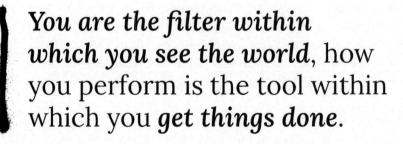

INTRODUCTION

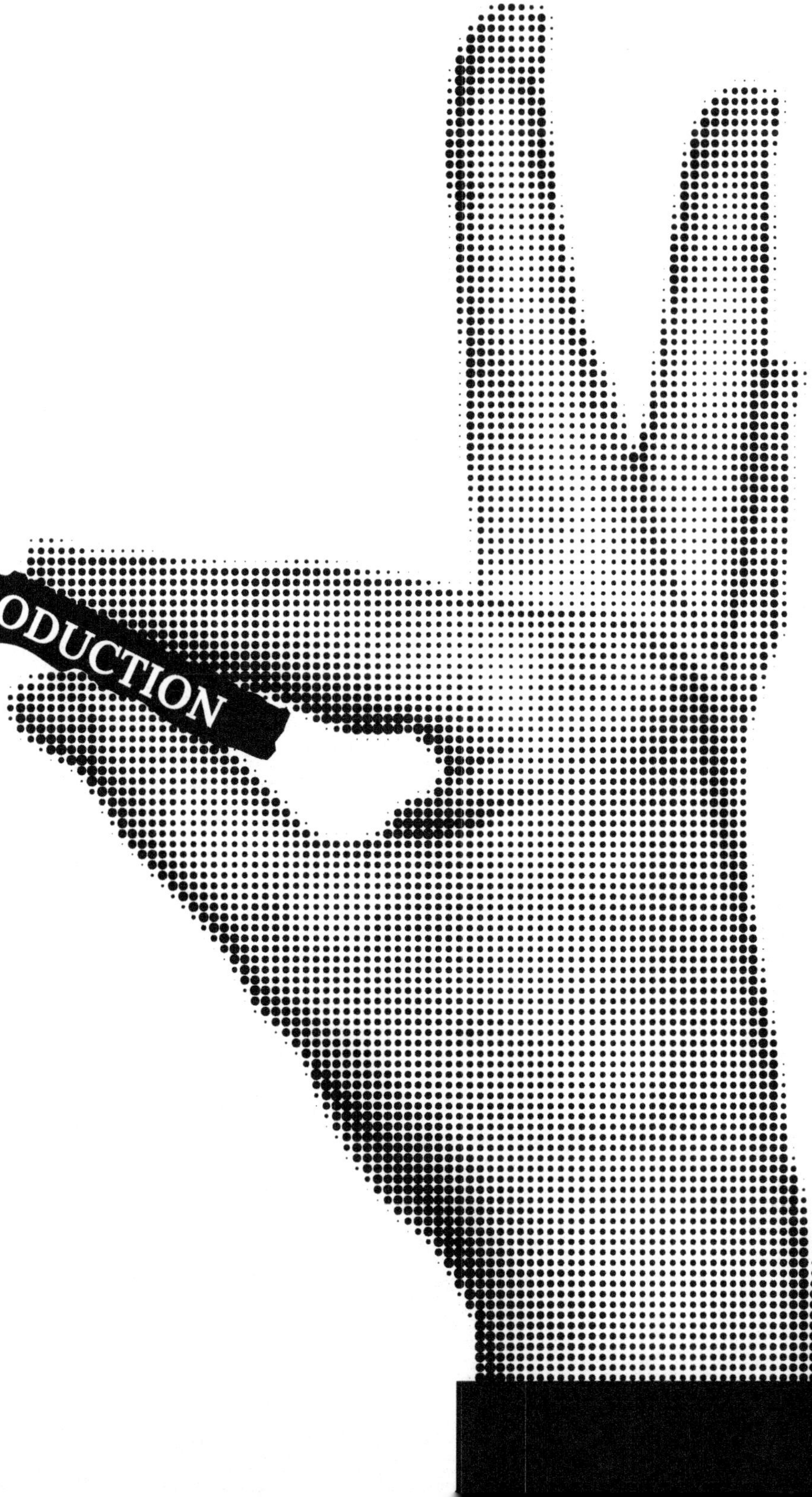

INTRODUCTION

At any given moment, we are on a constant treadmill requiring sustained effort to achieve anything of greatness. Always looking for tools that help this be achieved. Learning from others is a time-old tradition, which we then layer with our own life lessons and experience to create how we choose to approach life and success. To ultimately become the best versions of ourselves.

This book is about sharing years of experience of working with high achievers has created and lessons learned from others and myself, to bring about an understanding of how it is possible. As with anything, this requires work, however first of all an awareness. An awareness of what needs to be considered and why, the best ways to approach this and most importantly maintain, improve and review.

The overall framework and thinking behind this book is a melting pot of my learnings from earlier days working in fitness training, mindset and peak performance as an Neuro Linguistic Programming coach with Traders to scaling hundreds of businesses and coaching successful individuals who were performing at peak or if not I took them there.

"Take your sh!t to the next level" acts as your toolkit to understand how to become the best version of yourself and what you need to do to get there. The fundamentals of this book invite you to commit to continuous improvement and growth, bridging the gap between where you are and where you want to be. Full of tried-and-tested techniques and insights, this book offers practical guidance for success in both work and life.

Whether you're an entrepreneur looking to take yourself to the next level, a professional looking to raise their game, or an individual committed to personal development, this book arms you with the tools necessary to make that a success and become the best version of yourself. From mastering the art of time management to developing a resilient mindset, each chapter presents insights and actionable tips to add to your toolkit.

We kick off with the 'Framework' which has been structured as each of the chapters. Highlighting the three main key aspects required at the core and the foundation to maintain these. At the end of each chapter is 'how to get your sh!t sorted' a space to remind of the key takeaways, 'digging deeper' questions that will elicit further thinking and finally a space for you to make any notes.

The cool part is towards the back of the book where we delve into the 'improving' and 'measuring' chapters, which you can use as ways to do just that. Take your time with each chapter and allow yourself to create new sustained thinking and habits from each part. It's been written in such a way that you can revisit and remind yourself at any stage.

I have written this book in my own style. Sometimes direct and to the point, other times reflective (as in this section) or with authentic and open anecdotes and lessons from my own journey, with pepperings of my dyslexia just to add flavour. I hope that you get as much out of this as I did writing it.

So, are you ready to get your sh!t together?

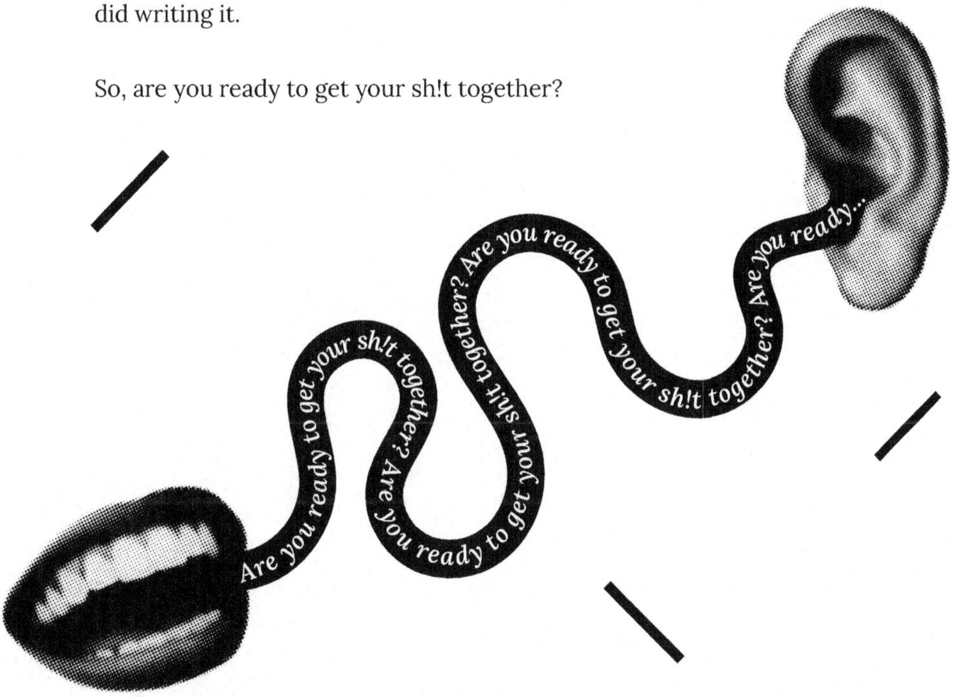

CHAPTER 1

The best version of you

CHAPTER 1

THE BEST VERSION OF YOU

This chapter shows the importance of being the best version of yourself to achieve success, including the key aspects to consider such as physical fitness, mindset, and energy states. Highlighting the foundational elements which sustain these areas including habits, actions, consistency, and interdependence. By maintaining the right habits, consistent action and an awareness on how to improve overall, we are able to substantially raise the bar on how we perform day to day, leading to accelerated growth and success in life.

To make the most of every opportunity, personally and professionally it is about keeping the bar high with how you show up, who you are and how you function. The best version of yourself. This is fundamental to success, and those who have achieved this, they got this part right.

We've seen lots of versions of what great looks like, from extreme daily routines to advice around what you should do to remain your best. The overall framework and thinking behind this book I've taken from my learnings as a fitness personal trainer, working with mindset as an NLP Coach, alongside entrepreneurs and helping highly driven people to get shit done and show up in the right way.

It all starts with focusing on your physical fitness and well-being, mindset and energy management. The key aspects that support your growth. From there we look at sustaining these through the development of habits and the right consistent actions. Understanding yourself and then mastering time management are what you then do with this solid base. Finally, continuous improvement and measurement ensure that you're always moving forwards and growing.

At the heart of "*Time to Get Your Sh!t Together*" lies a framework that supports this. The diagram on the next page outlines the main areas we'll explore throughout this book:

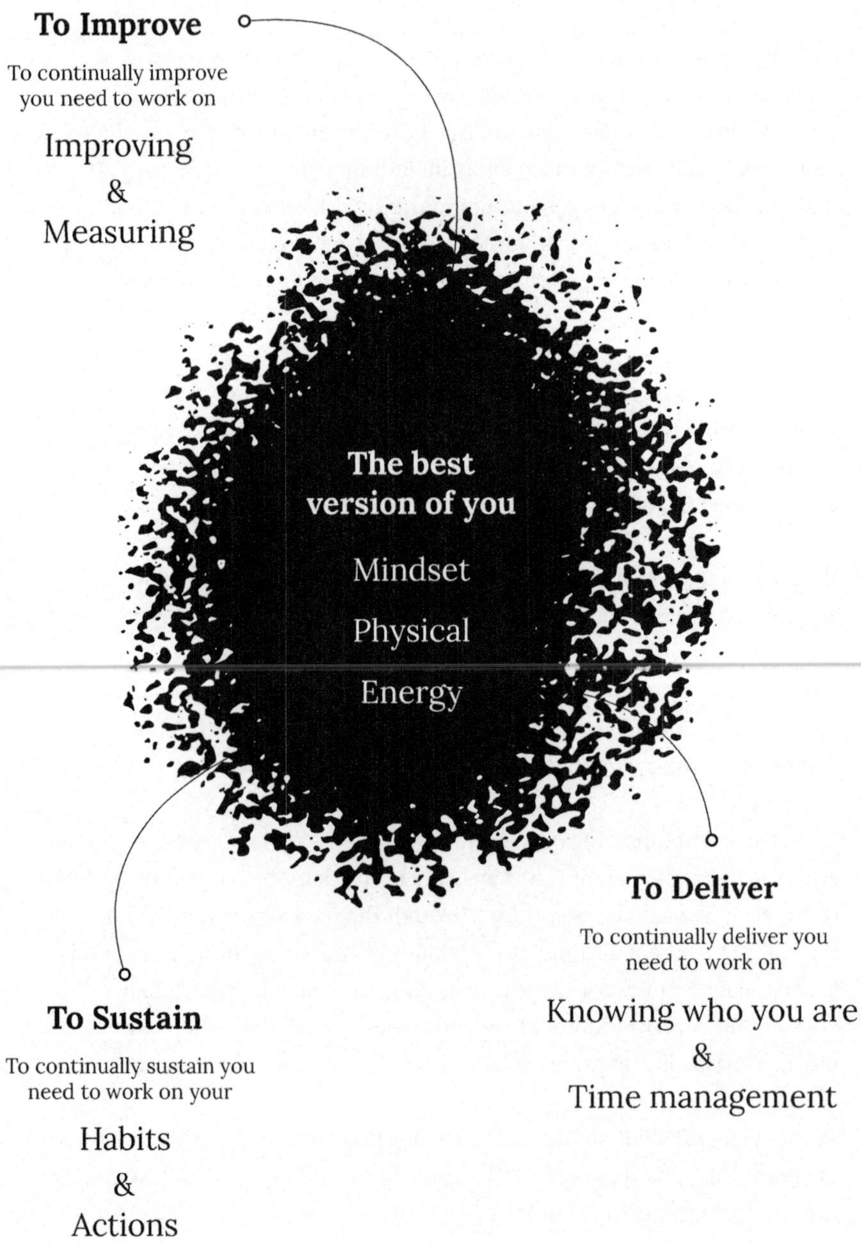
To Improve
To continually improve you need to work on
Improving
&
Measuring
The best version of you
Mindset
Physical
Energy
To Deliver
To continually deliver you need to work on
Knowing who you are
&
Time management
To Sustain
To continually sustain you need to work on your
Habits
&
Actions

Don't
half mast
it, pull your
finger out and
show them why
it should be
you.

Physical

I've had the fortune in my earlier years to have studied anatomy and physiology and become a personal trainer and aerobics teacher successfully training clients in Central London for over 5 years. The main take away from this was the importance of maintaining your physical fitness and how this impacts our life. And that in order to achieve success, we need to aim for the highest level of physical fitness that we are able to get to individually as a non-negotiable.

How fit you are not only directly impacts your performance but also how good or bad we feel about yourself at that time. If you can't be bothered to train, how do you think that you are going to achieve true success? People don't become successful by not bothering to get up or get on with something. Even if you gloss it over, right at the back of your mind you will not be achieving what you need to, altering how you think and feel.

So often we focus on the physical aspect and how that makes us feel. But how we are managing our fitness and our relationship with it also has an impact on us. Athletes train with sports specific training to achieve what they need to, so it makes sense that to be the best version of yourself and at peak performance that you should do the same.

On my own journey, I have found that being fit and maintaining a solid fitness regime has been the difference between either maintaining success or getting through a hard time and, well, not.

The simple fact is that if you want to have a healthy and long life you need to maintain your fitness to a level that can help you attain that. For those that want to be able to function as the best version of themselves, you need to be at your peak fitness at any given moment.

Being physically fit maintains and improves cognitive function, energy levels, mental health and overall well-being. Other benefits include a reduction in the risk of chronic diseases such as heart disease, diabetes and certain cancers. Now this isn't about being Triathlon ready, it's about having the key areas of fitness covered and maintaining them.

Alongside this is the need for a healthy balanced diet in order to 'feed the machine'. Ever heard the phrase you are what you eat? This could not be more true. Now I am not going to attempt to go in to specifics around the food and diet options in this book, as this is the one area I am not an expert in, however in order to achieve the physical aspect your diet must be balanced and healthy and one that suits your needs at that time.

This impacts how you feel and how you show up. From my experience, it is what we eat and our relationship with food that impacts our actions; now this I will explore later on in this book.

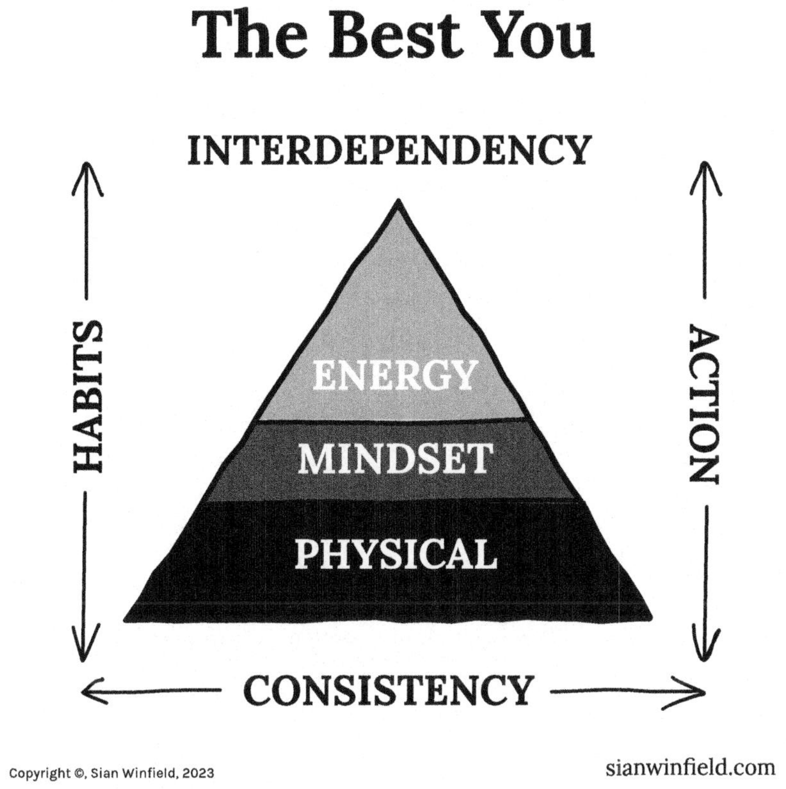

Mindset

Following the successful stint working in the fitness industry, I was fascinated about the fact that some of the people that I was training would just not stick or maintain what they needed to do. Now you are talking about the majority of my clients having been CEO, Traders or top executives. I just couldn't wrap my head around it. Surely if they wanted to be successful they would maintain the one aspect that helps them?

I had heard about NLP at the time, Neurolinguistic Programming, the art and science of communication. The ability to be able to further understand and interact with others and how it can be used to substantially elevate your game.

NLP offers a transformative approach to interaction and growth. Its essence lies in its toolkit, enabling individuals to build rapid rapport, sharpen their awareness of verbal and non-verbal cues and understand how to adapt communication styles to improve the probability of achieving desired outcomes for themselves or others. Pretty cool stuff!

After successfully studying and applying these principles to my clients' training, I was asked to design a training course for a trading company inspired by a renowned book on NLP for Traders and Investors. Learning to trade and rolling this out fed my fascination with peak performance, for sure.

Now, do remember that back then (20 odd years ago) their mindset and subsequent aligned strategies required an exceptionally high level of mental agility and focus. They didn't have the luxury of the amount of AI and technology used in trading these days to ensure that they stayed on track and so the importance of maintaining focus and cognitive function was an absolute must.

Your mindset is key to ensuring you're functioning in the right space to be the best version of yourself and see the best ways to tap into that.

Energy

Now, let's delve into the concept of energy from a multifaceted point of view.

It's not just about the type of energy you use day-to-day, it's also about being aware of how you interact with others and the energy you project, which significantly influences your outcomes.

A key issue contributing to an individual or team underperforming often comes from tapping into the wrong type of energy to function day to day. This can come from negative motivation, limited mindset, previous hardship and trauma or ingrained habits. Operating in this survival mode or lingering in it gives a ceiling on what can be achieved, leading to burnout, mental health concerns or a repeated pattern of limited success.

My own experience of functioning in survival mode, triggered by my earlier years, meant that it wasn't until I shifted from 'survive' to 'thrive' that real movement forward and the opportunity for success was found. I liken it to hanging on to a cliff even when you now have a solid ledge beneath you. You can let go; you just need to see that you can.

Then there's the energy we give out at any given time. Have you heard the saying 'you get back what you give out'? This couldn't be more true. Many successful leaders, despite questionable qualifications, become successful through sheer confidence and the energy surrounding their success that they give out.

Positive and negative energy also impacts various aspects of life. How we manage and interact with this determines the impact we allow it to have on us. You will see now how fundamental this aspect is to becoming the best version of yourself.

The foundation of the best version of you

In order to be functioning at our peak we need to establish the right foundations to maintain the key aspects through intentional actions, positive habits and consistent behaviours.

These elements are another non-negotiable in my opinion. Otherwise you just have a bunch of stuff that you are doing but not keeping up.

Habits

So here's the first of the elements that help us maintain the three key aspects. The right habits that keep the right levels going. We have habits that maintain who we are (whether that be where we want to be or not) and habits that create the world around us, help us grow, move forwards and improve who we are.

Most people are aware of how hard it is to maintain the right habits and level of maintenance consistently over time. Culturally, we even have new year's resolutions which come from this very fact. Having great habits requires making sure that all your habits serve you. Unless you are already thriving with great results, it is fair to say that the prospect of this could feel overwhelming.

The main learning here is that we are in control of our habits and can shape our life into whatever we choose it to be. Yes, we all swing to and fro between good and bad habits however with conscious effort you can improve these with a massive positive effect overall.

I've had the fortune of working with some absolutely outstanding entrepreneurs who have set the bar high in terms of their habits and routines that enable them to function at that level.

The higher the percentage of good habits that serve you and where you want to be heading, the happier, more fulfilled and motivated you are.

When we have a lower percentage of good habits or more bad ones, we go off track, are hard on ourselves and tend to repeat the cycle unless it is broken.

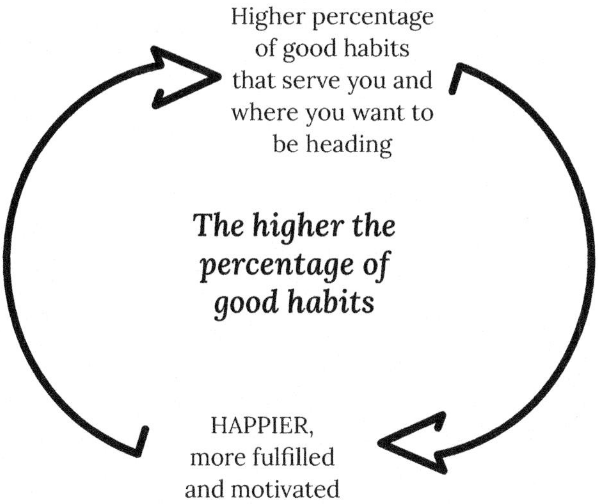
Higher percentage of good habits that serve you and where you want to be heading
The higher the percentage of good habits
HAPPIER, more fulfilled and motivated

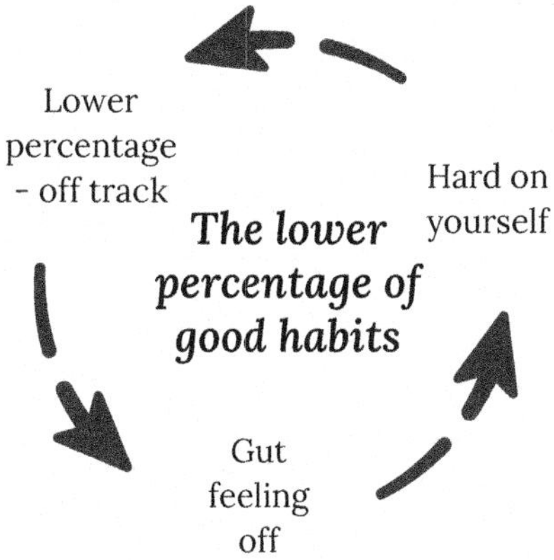
Lower percentage - off track
The lower percentage of good habits
Hard on yourself
Gut feeling off

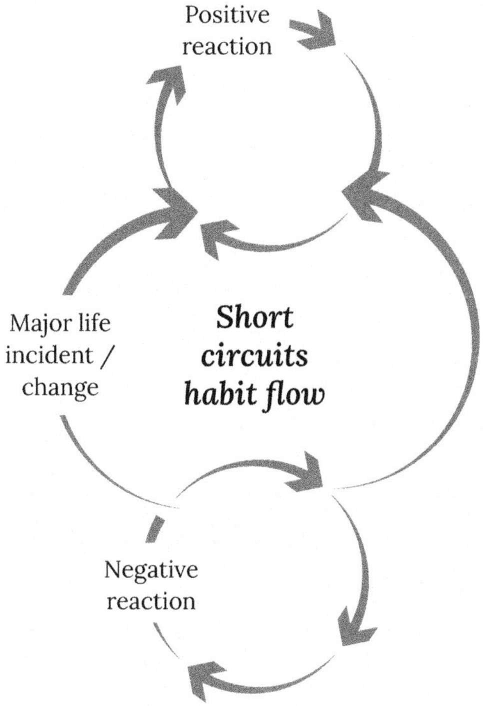
Positive reaction
Major life incident / change
Short circuits habit flow
Negative reaction

The habit cycle

It is only when for most there is a major life incident or change that this then short circuits the habit flow and we are then able to change cycle. If it is a good reaction then it is a positive cycle we head into or we can equally have a turn on to the bad habit cycle.

Believe it or not you can actively define the habits that you want to have to create the life you want. I've both seen it and done it. It takes only 21 days for the majority of people to make a habit and 90 days to make it a permanent lifestyle change.

The exciting thing is that when you are using the right habits that support the aspects of physical, mindset and energy you can actually get tangible results pretty quickly that will spur you on.

Action

Every action you take shapes your reality in life, in business or any area. Taking intentional actions sustain movement towards becoming your best self. Constant movement forwards is needed to drive any type of significant progress.

While it may seem obvious, it's the things that we don't actually get around to doing that have the biggest impact on us. These hold us back from being in the place we could really be in. Leading to a lack of growth or even sabotaging our own efforts.

We need actions that not only maintain but also shape our present and future lives. Each choice, each action, each deliberate step forwards creates either a positive or negative outcome. The connection between choice, action and outcome cannot be overstated. It's a continuous cycle where decisions and actions shape the results we experience. The key lies in the choice.

Alongside the previous points is the importance of spending time on the right things. Clearly aligned actions should support the delivery of your overall objectives by making sure that you are clear about why, what, and when you invest your time in to reach your goals. This ensures that you are always heading in the right direction.

From my experience the reason why an individual or business is successful, comes down to the actions they take or don't take. We go more into this in the main chapter.

Consistency

Unlike the earlier sections of this chapter, I don't go into this topic in a future chapter so for this section and the one following on interdependence, I'm going to go a bit deeper.

Consistency is the foundation upon which success is built. It's the persistent effort over time that brings epic results, as every action if maintained consistently means that you will inevitably get to where you are looking to go. Maintaining consistency in what we are looking to do can be challenging even for those aware of its importance. Things get in the way, we change or life events happen or we just lose interest. Bringing about repeated patterns of being on and off track.

The true power of consistency lies in its ability to tap into the compound effect, where small actions accumulate to produce exponential growth. Much like compounding interest, the benefits of consistent effort build up gradually but steadily over time leading to serious progress.

This is massively significant in becoming or maintaining the best version of yourself. There is a big impact on your life when making smart choices on a daily basis and the growth this can lead to. By committing to daily, consistent and disciplined action it is entirely possible to unlock the potential for profound growth while not feeling like you are doing a lot. Crazy.

Consider the example of Serena Williams, one of the greatest tennis players of all time. Throughout her career, Serena has shown unwavering consistency in her training, matches, and mindset. Serena's success is not just down to her natural talent but also to her dedication to consistency.

She maintains a relentless training programme, a strict fitness routine, and consistently works on fine-tuning her skills and strategy on the court. Despite facing setbacks and challenges, Serena's commitment to consistency has enabled her to win numerous Grand Slam titles and Olympic gold medals. Her ability to consistently perform at a high level, match after match and year after year, demonstrates the power of consistency in achieving her success. An example of how dedication to consistency can massively elevate performance.

The impact of consistency on growth over time

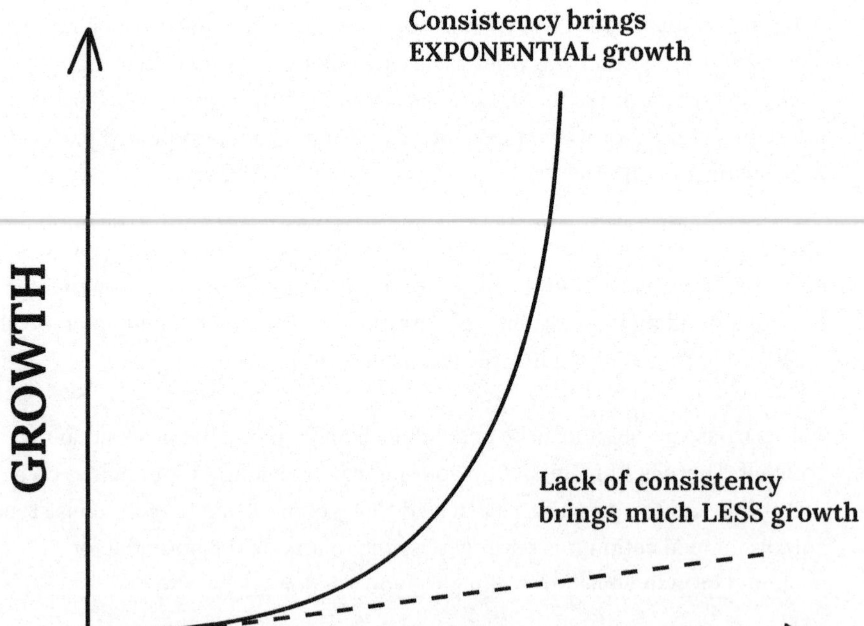

So what can you do to be more consistent?

Understand that you need to shift your mindset for whatever you are looking to do to become a long-term change rather than something temporary. To become a habit. Commit to the change permanently.

Along the way when approaching challenges to consistency you need to develop strategies to keep up with what you need to do such as accountability partners, habit tracking and resilience-building techniques aligned with what you are looking to maintain. That can also be achieved by reducing or increasing time spent or the level of what you are keeping up to be able to maintain it. Be kind when needed, celebrate small wins along the way, to maintain motivation and reinforce positive actions. Consistency requires measuring and keeping on track. Reflecting on your progress, identifying areas for improvement and making the required changes. We cover this further in Chapter 8.

And finally, for anything that you are looking to do or maintain long-term you must be massively committed, driven and inspired to achieve it, or at least get to the point where it is a habit and you can see and appreciate the benefit.

> You only have one life so *it's entirely up to you* whether you nail it or not. *Really.*

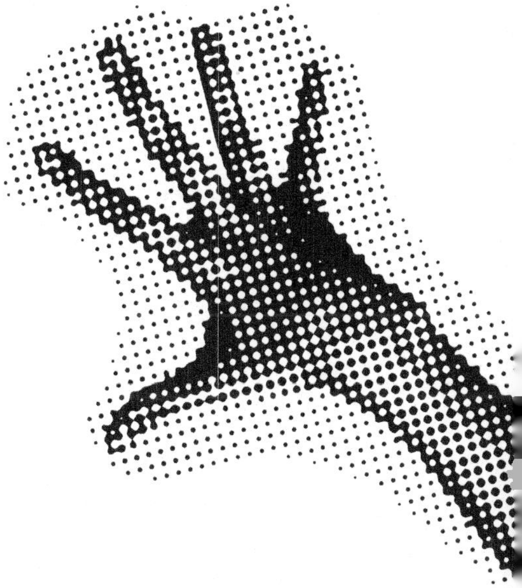

Interdependency

The final aspect to this framework is Interdependence. While it may not usually be in this sort of conversation, it's important to ensure that once you've reached the best version of yourself, that you engage with others to make the most of that opportunity. Otherwise quite frankly you limit yourself to just your own circle of influence. Interdependence is the interconnectedness between people. No one operates in isolation and as such real success comes from meaningful connections with others, collaborations and support networks.

Embracing interdependence involves realising the advantage of relationships, the guidance and power of community that amplifies achievements and approaching challenges effectively. Essentially, it's recognising that our ability to thrive is enhanced through mutually beneficial relationships. A collective effort toward shared goals. Advantages include:

- *Shared resources*
  Interdependence allows the sharing of resources, knowledge and skills. With the advantage of collaboration and collective problem-solving. We don't have all the answers or know everything, so having a large network of relationships you can tap into is a powerful place to be.

- *Diverse perspectives*
  Engaging with diverse viewpoints broadens understanding and provides fresh insights to increase personal growth. It stops the lack of diverse thinking and creates space for us to really see what we have around us. What we are looking to do and be challenged when needed. A great example of another level of support to the 3 main aspects physical fitness, mindset development and energy. Helping to highlight new ideas and strategies to further improve these areas.

- *Accountability and motivation*
  Interdependence creates accountability and motivation as individuals support each other. Helping to staying committed to their end goal through increased networks of like-minded individuals. These can be used as accountability partners and support groups. To be able to take what you are looking to do so much further than if you were doing it alone.

- *Synergy and innovation*
  Collaborative thinking and effort often leads to aligned outcomes and increased opportunity. For innovation, creativity and the generation of new ideas creates huge momentum forwards. Thinking and ideas that are just not possible on our own.

- *Resilience and adaptability*
  Interdependence improves resilience and adaptability by providing a support network during challenging times. Offering encouragement and alternative perspectives and strategies for bouncing back stronger.

- *Independence as the foundation*
  From my own experience growing up having left home at a young age, I found that I became very independent. In fact. I would say that for many years I was too independent with almost an inability to ask for help and a solo player mentality. While it is great to be independent and strong, it is also important to ensure that you are not pushing others away. Missing opportunities by going too far into that zone is not ideal.

  If you are overly independent, it really does limit the potential of what you are able to achieve. Getting the balance between the two, now that is exactly where you want to be! It's important to ensure that you strike the balance between being independent and interdependent, both powerful skills to possess.

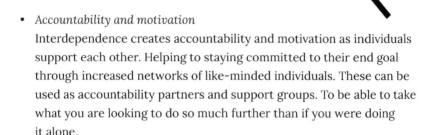

Essentially, it's recognising that our ability to thrive is enhanced through mutually beneficial relationships. A collective effort toward shared goals.

The path from independence to interdependence

The diagram below illustrates the journey from independence to interdependence. The attributes associated with each stage indicated with the arrows signify the progression.

Key attributes in 'be independent' like initiative, determination and self-discipline are fundamental to success. These attributes are action-oriented and enable individuals to achieve huge amounts independently.

Interestingly, it Is then the other attributes in the 'be smart' and 'be savvy' sections, such as critical thinking, problem-solving, resourcefulness and adaptability that enable progress. We don't often ponder these areas, however when you do start to think about these, you are enabling yourself to add these to your toolkit. Increasing the ability to see where you are lacking and where you need to grow.

Reflecting on these attributes, consider how many you currently have or use. Does this prompt any self-reflection about those around you or your current team and areas for improvement or development?

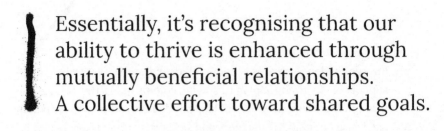

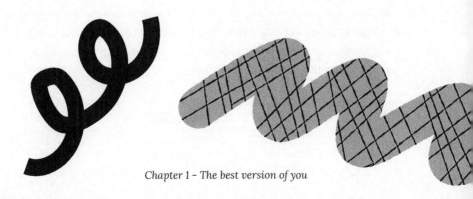

The path from independence to interdependence

Be Independent		**Be Smart**		**Be Savvy**		**Be Interdependent**
Self-reliance	→	*Knowledge*	→	*Resourcefulness*	→	*Collaboration*
Initiative		*Critical-thinking*		*Adaptability*		*Communication*
Determination		*Problem-solving*		*Networking*		*Teamwork*
Goal-setting		*Learning mindset*		*Creativity*		*Mutual support*
Self-discipline				*Strategic thinking*		*Synergy*

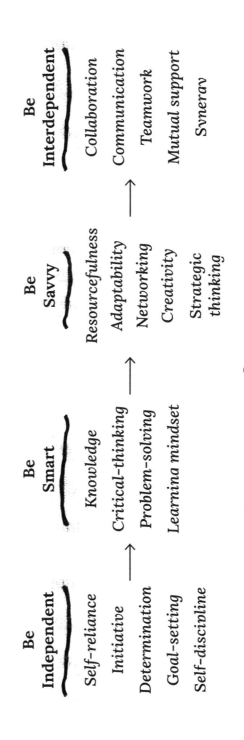

How to get your sh!t sorted

The best version of you

- Being the best version of yourself involves maintaining physical fitness, your mindset and being at peak at any given moment. Managing energy effectively in different scenarios are the key aspects and consistency in habits and actions is crucial for sustainable progress. Making growth in these areas at the level required.

- Recognise the value interconnectedness, interdependence and a wider network creates to support your success. Achieving growth between independence and interdependence and the understanding of key attributes required is essential.

- The journey towards the best version of oneself requires self-reflection, intentional choices and a commitment to continuous improvement. It is an investment to get this right however, nothing great comes easily!

Digging Deeper

The best version of you

- Rate out of 10 where you are currently with physical fitness, mindset and energy consistency.

- What does being the best version of yourself mean to me, considering the aspects of physical fitness, mindset and energy states?

- How do my current habits and actions align with my vision of the best version of myself? What changes do I need to make?

- What role does consistency play in currently achieving my goals across the areas of physical fitness, mindset development and energy management? What do I need to do more or less of?

- How can I create an awareness of where I sit between independence and interdependence? Using the path diagram, what do I yet need to do more of in terms of missing attributes?

- How am I currently utilising interdependence in my personal and professional life to enhance growth and success? Do I need to do this more? How can I do that?

Notes, musings and thoughts to myself

(Use these pages to make notes on what you've read to help get your sh!t together)

CHAPTER 2

The best version of you: Physical

CHAPTER 2
PHYSICAL

This chapter stresses the importance of physical fitness for overall performance alongside this, highlighting the significance of a balanced, healthy diet.

It demonstrates how these choices impact energy levels, mood, and overall well-being. Showcasing the effects of habit consistency in these areas, from increased energy to better mood regulation.

Additionally, this chapter encourages readers to reflect on their own fitness and dietary habits. Learning to take actionable steps towards healthier, enhanced performance and well-being.

How many summers do you have left?

Make them count.

Your fitness

The simple fact is that if you want to lead a healthy and long life, you need to maintain your fitness. At a level that can help you perform at your best at any given moment. Switched on and thinking clearly. I once heard someone say that to really see where you are, you need to ask yourself 'how many summers do I have left?' This really brings home not only how short life is, but how important it is to stay well and mobile for as long as possible.

Being fit and maintaining a solid fitness regime is also the difference between either maintaining success or getting through a hard time and well, not. I spent many years training senior executives and traders in London city, all of whom were really tapping into the benefit of being physically fit. Getting the advantage in the highly competitive landscape that they were working in.

Now, this isn't about being Triathlon-ready; it's about covering the key areas of fitness and maintaining them. So, how much should you be doing? According to guidelines from the Chief Medical Officers (CMOs) of the four UK nations, adults aged 19-64 should aim to achieve at least 150 minutes of moderate-intensity aerobic activity or 75 minutes of vigorous-intensity aerobic activity per week. Additionally, it's recommended to mix this with muscle-strengthening activities on two or more days a week.

The recommended percentage of time to spend on each aspect of physical well being really does vary based on individual goals, fitness levels, and preferences. However, here's a guideline for maintaining overall physical health. Showing how to tap into those particular types of fitness and the percentage of recommended time split in your workouts.

These percentages can be adjusted based on individual preferences, fitness goals and specific needs. If you are also doing sports specific training then this is more often than not leaning more towards the attributes needed in that area.

Recommended time split between fitness types

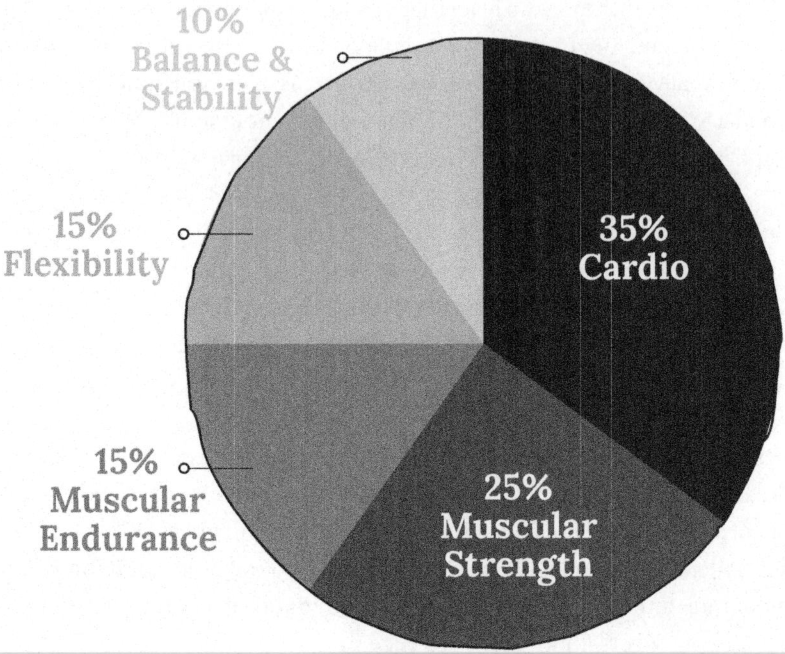

Cardio

Why this rocks:
Endurance

Recommended allocation:
Aim for about 30-40% of your exercise time.

Benefits:

- Improved heart health
- Increased lung capacity
- Weight management
- Improved mood
- Better sleep
- Increased energy
- Improved metabolism
- Reduced risk of chronic diseases
- Increased endurance and stamina
- Better cognitive function
- Improved ability to get through long days

Types of training:
Too many to list here.... running, bike, gym cardio equipment right through to walking.

Muscular Strength

Think weight trainer/ bulk muscle mass

Why this rocks:
Strength and body composition

Recommended allocation:
Aim for 20-30% of your exercise time.

Benefits:

- Increased muscle mass
- Enhanced muscle strength
- Improved muscle tone
- Better posture
- Enhanced joint stability
- Reduced risk of injury
- Improved metabolism
- Enhanced athletic performance
- Increased bone density
- Stronger day to day

Types of training:
Free weights or weight bearing resistance machines, body with exercises (push ups, press ups etc) Gym classes catered around these.
*The key is **heavier weights, lower reps***

Muscular Endurance

Think marathon runner/ lean muscle mass

Why this rocks:
Endurance and muscle composition

Recommended allocation:
Aim for 10-20% of your exercise time.

Such as high-repetition weightlifting or bodyweight exercises.

Benefits:

- Prolonged muscular endurance
- Enhanced resistance to fatigue
- Improved stamina during physical activity
- Better performance in endurance sports
- Increased ability to sustain repetitive movements
- Enhanced cardiovascular efficiency
- Reduced risk of muscular cramps and strains
- Improved recovery time between workouts
- Enhanced overall physical performance
- Better functional capacity in daily activities
- Ability to maintain tasks and activities for longer

Types of training:
Free weights or weight bearing resistance machines,
body with exercises (push ups, press ups etc) Gym classes catered around these.
*The key is **lower weights**, **multiple reps**.*

Flexibility

Why this rocks:
Mobility

Benefits:

- Better range of motion in joints
- Enhanced muscle elasticity
- Improved posture and alignment
- Reduced risk of injury
- Better athletic performance
- Enhanced coordination and balance
- Reduced muscle tension and stiffness
- Improved circulation
- Enhanced relaxation and stress relief
- Better overall mobility
- Less likely to have an injury or get cramp running around

Recommended allocation:
Aim for about 10-20% of your exercise time.

Types of training:
From yoga to stretch to Pilates there are many classes and types of fitness that help with this

Balance and Stability

Why this rocks:
Core balance, posture

Benefits:

- Better balance
- Good stability
- Better coordination
- Reduced risk of injuries
- Improved body awareness
- Increased core strength
- Improved posture
- Better athletic performance
- Enhanced agility
- Increased confidence in movement
- Steadier stance and management of running around day to day

Recommended allocation:
Aim for about 5-10% of your exercise time.

Types of training:
This again could include from yoga to stretch to Pilates style classes or training.

Picking the right type of fitness that motivates you or you enjoy is the foundation of any successfully maintained workout plan. What do you currently do? Is it working for you? If not, what do you need to change?

Every day is
a new start.

Make today
epic.

Making it work for you

So this is all great to read, but what if you're super busy and just don't have the time? Not a good enough excuse. A busy diary often makes it challenging to fit in exercise but the ironic part is that in order to keep those diaries full and perform well to create and manage your workload, you need to find time to stay physically fit. There are practical ways to fit it into our day.

When my son was younger and needed a lot of my time and I was also setting up my company, it was really difficult to get fitness into my day. Today, I have a spinning bike at home along with resistance bands, and you can often find me jumping on the bike in between Zoom calls or at the beginning or end of the day. And a money saver for sure! Here are a few strategies to help you fit that all-important fitness into your routine.

Bring fitness to you

One approach is to bring fitness to you by choosing a workout that can be done at home or at your office. Bodyweight exercises, yoga routines, or using resistance bands are great options that require minimal equipment and space. By removing the need to travel to a gym, you can save time and bring workouts into your day. Try HIIT workouts (high intensity) 30-minute mini circuits. Taking up less time, burning more fat and getting you in the right headspace as you blast out your favourite music. The added benefit of a mood changer.

Plan it properly

Another strategy is to make sure that you actually plan dedicated time for exercise in your diary. By blocking out specific time slots and treating them as non-negotiable, you're more likely to fit in those regular workouts and set yourself accountability. Just don't get used to moving them unless absolutely necessary, get used to doing them as a habit and you bring in the feel-good vibe from that too. In fact consistent, shorter workouts will get you better long-term results because you have stuck with it rather than intensive sessions for a while and then just giving up.

Bring movement to your day

Finding opportunities to bring more movement into your day-to-day can add to your overall fitness too. Walking more, taking short exercise breaks during work or choosing the stairs instead of lifts. These are simple yet effective ways to stay active throughout the day. By combining exercise with other tasks like listening to podcasts or standing up while working, you increase the amount of time you are keeping your body physically fit. With these practical strategies, staying active becomes more achievable even if you are super busy.

Set a fitness target

Most people are motivated by a target, a single point that motivates them to complete the task at hand. I've seen many people drop off their fitness because they see the target as 'getting to the gym after working all day'. That's like trying to be motivated by completing an Excel spreadsheet at work rather than the why of the business or the project at hand. Whereas a motivator of looking and feeling great by X day as an example, actually will ultimately motivate you more. What is your real motivator to working out or getting fit and how can you use that to stick with it?

Already pretty fit?

For those who are already fit, it is about not only improving fitness but ensuring that you stay engaged and interested. Create and plan for the next stage of training and how to elevate that. If you need help, the fitness professionals at your local gym should easily be able to review where you are and how to take it to the next level. Fitness and physical health can always be improved and challenged.

Ask yourself whether your routine is fully balanced? So often when you have individuals who are very fit, they often do this to the detriment of flexibility which actually can help you become an even better athlete. Especially due to the increased range of muscle motion, reduced recovery time and reduced stress overall.

Ways to improve your physical fitness

So what about improving fitness as a whole? Here are your key pointers:

Keep it consistent

Maintain a consistent routine and vary the types of exercise such as cardio, strength training, flexibility, and balance exercises. Aim for at least 30 minutes of moderate-intensity exercise most days of the week, though start slowly and build up if needed.

Build it up

Establish achievable fitness goals that align with your current fitness level and long-term objectives. Break down larger goals into smaller, manageable milestones to track your progress and maintain motivation. Mix it up: Keep your workouts engaging and challenging by incorporating a variety of exercises and activities. Explore different fitness classes, outdoor activities, or sports to avoid boredom and maintain interest.

Learn

Educate yourself about different types of exercises and effective workout techniques. There is a wealth of information available online and in podcasts. Stay updated on the latest fitness trends, research, and recommendations to ensure your workouts yield optimal results.

Listen to your body

Pay attention to your body and adapt your workouts accordingly. If you feel excessively tired or if exercises feel too easy, make necessary adjustments by resting or increasing intensity. Stay in touch with your body's signals. Allow for rest and recovery days to prevent overtraining and minimise the risk of injury. Bring in stretching when necessary to enhance flexibility and alleviate muscle tension.

Track your progress

Track your workouts and achievements to stay motivated and accountable. Use fitness apps, a diary, or wearable fitness trackers to monitor your activity levels, establish new goals, and celebrate your accomplishments. There's an exercise at the end of this chapter designed to help you stay on top of your physical performance on a day-to-day basis.

Tracking physical well-being exercise

To track your physical fitness throughout the day, it's essential to assess how you feel physically and your activities. Here's an exercise that can help you track and review your physical well-being and your day-to-day ability to function.

By following these simple steps you can better understand and improve your physical well-being. As with any tracking tool, you need to first see what you are doing (we so often forget or fib to ourselves). Then improve on that. It is recommended to keep this up for at least a month to see the real benefit from it and to meet both the habit-making mark. Then to start to feel the benefits to keep you going.

Consistency exercise: physical

With consistency being a fundamental part of the successful implementation of fitness into your routine, this table enables you to track this. A very simple yet effective exercise, the key is sticking to it and completing it all.

See the table on the next page. In 'Days of the week' add in your chosen fitness into the days right the way across the six weeks, ensuring that you make it feasible. You then cross out when each one is completed. The minimum suggested duration to do this is six weeks, by which time you should be both experiencing the benefits and have maintained this as a habit.

The fun part? You can use this consistency exercise for any habit that you are looking to maintain. Repeating the six-week cycle to bring exercise into your routine and then maintain it in the longer term.

Week	Monday	Tuesday	Wednesday	Thursday	Friday	Saturday	Sunday
1	Bike	Squats	Bike	Squats	Weights	Run	Bike
2	Squats	Run	Bike		Weights		Bike
3							
4							
5							
6							

Track your progress

- Keep It Regular
  Track your well-being daily over a few weeks minimum.

- Be Honest
  Rate your energy and discomfort openly.

- Add Details
  Include specifics about your activities and their duration.

- Set Realistic Goals
  Make achievable goals based on what you observe.

- Spot Patterns
  Look for connections between your activities and how you feel.

- Make Adjustments
  Use your learnings to adjust your routine as needed.

- Stay Flexible
  Be open to changing your tracking method if necessary.

Know your worth,

don't settle for second best.

How to get your sh!t sorted

The best version of you: Physical

- Physical fitness is essential for overall well-being and performance in all aspects of your life.
  Don't underestimate that.

- Maintain a balanced approach to exercise, focusing on key areas such as cardiovascular endurance, muscular strength, flexibility, balance and mobility.
  Across the board.

- Have a toolkit of practical strategies to help you overcome common barriers to physical fitness. Such as making sure you have time or ways to motivate yourself to help keep you on track.

- Consistency is a game-changer when it comes to physical exercise. With a huge amount of benefits from the regularity over a stop-and-start approach that you just don't keep up.

- By bringing in movement and smart ways to keep moving into your day, you can keep active without it being just the obvious idea of training and working out.

Digging deeper

The best version of you: Physical

- How do I currently fit exercise in my day or week?
- Am I happy with my level of physical activity and overall health? What do I need to do to improve it?
- If I am hammering it with a high level of physical fitness, is it balanced? How can I raise the bar yet again?
- What are the key barriers preventing me from bringing more physical activity into my week?
- How am I performing day to day? Do I think I need to improve my fitness to perform better in my day generally?
- How can I redefine my approach to fitness to make it more sustainable and enjoyable?
- What small changes can I make to bring more movement into my daily activities?

It's not just your physical health that's important, your diet is too, see overleaf!

Your Diet

Now as I mentioned I am not going to go into the specifics about food and diet options. Achieving physical wellness requires a balanced and healthy diet tailored to individual needs. Your diet hugely influences how you feel and how you present yourself. From personal experience our food choices and relationship with food significantly impact our actions. How we show up in the world and the level that we function at.

The link between food habits and overall health is undeniable. Eating the wrong foods not only affects our physical well-being but also influences our mood and decision-making abilities. Shaping the quality of life we lead and the heights we are able to reach.

Imagine removing unhealthy eating habits entirely. How would this impact your performance and mindset? For me this decision has been transformative.

The vast majority of people, myself included, switch back and forth between bouts of eating well and then not or drinking and then not. With an inconsistent routine around the food that they eat and their relationship with it.

As someone who focuses on continuously improving, I had been thinking for some time about the fact that I was in this silly dance with myself around food. The peaks and troughs of feeling good or bad surely impact the decisions we make and as such the life we create around us and the level we are able to get to?

They eat well and then feel good, eat that pizza or something sweet and then feel bad. Standard habits for a high % of us but what does that do to your mindset? How do you seize opportunities that day? Your focus and mood? Your health?

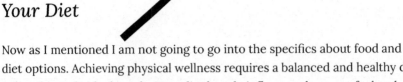

Making a change

It was 27th Feb 2022 just after the Ukrainian Russia war kicked off. At the time I was shocked and moved as many, many others were too and still are. It made me reflect on where my life was.

Compared to what those poor people were experiencing, there I was with the issue of not being able to get it together to eat consistently well. Poor western woman with first world problems. Something switched in me. It made me see the issue for what it was. Rubbish and completely pointless.

So I decided there and then: "I eat healthily". A complete and utter about turn and acceptance of the fact that this is who I now was. I was someone who eats healthily.

My diet shift mainly consisted of healthy, natural foods. I could eat anything that was fresh and natural. While I chose a vegetarian diet if it had contained meat the mindset shift would be similar and the benefits the same due to the consistency. 'Healthy' means anything natural so not having any unprocessed foods like takeaways, sweets, cakes, crisps, fizzy drinks, and other junk foods.

Loads of fruit, vegetables, and healthy snacks while occasionally indulging in a cocktail or two, for life balance! The key to success lies in consistency and the cumulative effect of sticking to this over time, resulting in habit changes that end up as a lifestyle choice resulting in long term health improvements.

This has now been maintained for over 2 years, with some of the benefits I didn't expect to experience. Benefits Included:

- Excellent focus, rarely get mentally tired
- No energy slumps
- No cravings for sweet or bad food
- Consistent moods
- Levelled up self-view (no time wasted at all on feeling bad about food choices)
- Calmer and more relaxed generally
- Improved sleep
- Better skin
- Improved gut health
- Improved body composition
- Weight loss
- Feeling and looking younger
- Money saved not buying rubbish food
- Improved sense of taste
- Increased ability to deal with stressful situations
- More confidence physically and mentally
- Better workouts / quicker recovery time

How to get your sh!t sorted

The best version of you: Physical (diet)

- Dietary habits massively influence physical and mental well-being, affecting energy levels, mood and overall health.
- Consistency in making healthy food choices over time can lead to profound transformations in various aspects of life.
- Eliminating processed foods, junk food and excess sugar from the diet can result in improved energy levels, better mood stability and enhanced cognitive function.
- Focussing on natural, unprocessed foods like fruits, vegetables, whole grains and lean proteins promotes overall health and supports physical fitness goals.
- Maintaining a balanced and healthy diet contributes to better sleep quality, improved skin health, enhanced gut health and increased resilience to stress.
- It's essential to be mindful of dietary choices and their impact on overall well-being. To make adjustments as needed to achieve optimal health and wellness.
- The benefits of a healthy diet extend far beyond physical health. To go on to impact mental clarity and your ability to function in your workplace and in other areas of your life.

Digging deeper

The best version of you: Physical (diet)

- How does my current diet support my goals for physical wellness?
- What are my main reasons for making dietary changes, if any?
- Am I mindful of how food choices impacts my energy levels, mood, and overall well-being?
- If eating the right food sets me on my game, what do I need to do better? More consistent?
- What are the biggest challenges I face in maintaining a healthy diet? How can I address them?
- What adjustments can I make to my dietary habits to better support my physical and mental health?

Notes, musings and thoughts to myself

(Use these pages to make notes on what you've read to help get your sh!t together)

Need more space? Here you go!

(Use these pages to make notes on what you've read to help get your sh!t together)

CHAPTER 3

The best version of you: Mindset

CHAPTER 3
MINDSET

In the mindset chapter, we dig into the influence of our thoughts and attitudes to our mindset. Through self-awareness and resilience we can shift challenges and learn to view setbacks as opportunities for growth. With practical strategies we create a positive outlook reframing negative thinking patterns to unlock our full potential for personal and professional growth.

To be the best version of yourself your mindset is key and you need to be functioning in the right headspace for success. Understanding the best ways to do this and tapping into the right thinking when needed.

We've all seen the 'wheel of life' which shows how where we spend our time dictates our sense of life balance and achievement. This sort of model could also be used for how we see the areas that we spend our time thinking about and also the type of mindset we allow ourselves to be in. We need it to be balanced and on the right things.

Your mind gets used to how you think and how we think is ultimately habitual, we get used to it. Therefore it requires conscious awareness of how you are using your mind and thinking to then improve on this. As with anything we do automatically we don't always see it. So we need to start to be aware day to day how we are functioning and notice the mindset states that we go into. Then deciding whether that state serves us or no
longer does.

When working with businesses to help them grow, I see that so often it is not just about having a clear strategy and direction but the way that the individual or team is thinking. Seeing what is going on and the types of mindset that they are in that dictates the success of a project or even the business. The very same can be said for how we approach our lives. So what do we need to be aware of in order to improve?

Why create problems in your head that don't even exist?

Types of mindsets

Growth mindset

To continue to grow you need to maintain a future focussed view.
To embrace a growth mindset that sees challenges as opportunities for learning and development. This thinking is one of the main contributors to success in our lives across the board.

A growth mindset embraces resilience, adaptability and a love of learning the new. While a fixed mindset massively inhibits personal development and ultimately overall potential. We can develop habits over time to put us into the growth mindset zone if this isn't natural or to help us maintain one.

Your path to a consistent growth mindset
The below represents best practices for maintaining a growth mindset. While they naturally make sense when we read them, keeping these in mind helps ensure that you maintain this thinking. Especially when faced with challenges.

- **See challenges as growth opportunities**
  Every challenge is a chance to learn and grow, not just a hurdle to overcome. Sh!t happens to everyone.

- **Effort leads to mastery**
  Understand that giving your energy into something offers an opportunity for learning and continuous improvement. Nothing great ever came easily.

- **Value feedback and criticism**
  Embrace feedback as insights for personal and professional development. However, remember that sometimes others' feedback tells you more about them than it does about you. Learn to hear, review and take action accordingly.

- **Inspiration from others' success**
  Let the success of others motivate you to reach higher and achieve more. There is more than enough room for everyone to achieve success in this world and for us all to be motivated by this.

- **Learn from setbacks**
  Every setback is a lesson and nothing more than a part of moving forwards, an opportunity to reassess and grow stronger. Learn, implement and move on.

- **Embrace continuous learning**
  Knowledge and continuous learning should be seen as a lifelong commitment to your personal and professional growth. There is just no excuse for not doing this now that we have so much at our fingertips.

Abundance mindset

Our mindset impacts what we see around us and our ability to not only spot opportunity but also to interact with it. So if we see abundance we are more likely to create more. And if our mindset is one of scarcity, our view and interactions will be the same regardless of it just being a filter or view.

The term "self-fulfilling prophecy" springs to mind. The sociologist Robert K. Merton introduced this in his work in 1948 in the "Social Theory and Social Structure." It describes the concept that individuals' beliefs and expectations directly influence our behaviour in a way that ultimately makes our expectations come true. And this is spot on.

Acknowledge and appreciate the abundance in your life and focus on what you have rather than what you don't. Bring this into your daily thinking. Look to maintain a positive outlook by believing in the abundance and huge amount of opportunities and resources around you. And you know what? If it isn't where it needs to be, allow yourself to feel that it is to create more of the same.

View setbacks as opportunities for growth and learning and continuously improve and any challenges with resilience and positive mindset knowing that every obstacle is short-term is learning.

Types of states

Now, underpinning the type of mindset overall are the types of states that we then function within. There could be an endless list here, however the one that I would like to highlight is the flow state. "In flow" is when you are completely engrossed and engaged in an activity creating a solid focus and deep involvement in the process.

This concept is penned by psychologist Mihaly Csikszentmihalyi and highlights the time when your skills perfectly match the level of challenge presented by what you are working on or creating. In this state, time seems to fade away as you become fully engrossed feeling a profound sense of satisfaction and accomplishment. It's that epic feeling of being in sync with what you're doing, where every moment feels purposeful and fulfilling.

Now, we can't always find this state, however what this highlights is that when you are working and functioning as your best self and in tune with the work that you are doing, this is when flow happens. Where you want to be. So if this is the case, what do you need to change in order for this to happen?

Keep your mind in check. Your thoughts create your world.

Types of Thinking

When we consider mindset we also need to look at the thinking patterns that influence how we approach tasks and challenges day to day. It's not just about having a positive mindset but understanding the different types of thinking we need to effectively accomplish our goals. In my experience coaching high achievers, the ability to seamlessly move between these different types of thinking and knowing what these are has been the difference between success and failure.

For example, leading a team in the early stages of a business requires a multifaceted approach. As a leader, you must not only grasp the roadmap and necessary actions but also take a step back to see the strategic angle. The ability to wear multiple hats at the same time, each with a different focus and perspective is so important. However challenges arise when individuals find themselves in roles that push them beyond their natural thinking abilities. The executives who excelled in corporate environments often fall short of the type of thinking needed in early-stage start-ups. Skills such as adaptability, creativity and resilience not often fostered or needed in a corporate setting.

On the other hand, some individuals thrive in the early stages of start-up growth, yet they may encounter issues as the business scales up. The shift towards establishing systems and processes to support growth is a mindset often overlooked in the early stages of entrepreneurship.

Ultimately, success hinges on the ability to recognise and adapt to the relevant thinking style or know when you need to either learn more or get someone who can support you in this. Being aware of when to zoom in on immediate tasks and when to zoom out to consider long-term strategies is super important. And creating a diverse range of thinking skills is essential for ensuring sustained growth and success.

Your thinking toolkit

Understanding the various types of thinking required for different situations is a game changer. Here's some of the different types:

- Strategic thinking
  Involves looking at the bigger picture, 'over the trees' and considering long-term goals and implications.

- Tactical thinking
  Focuses on the immediate actions and steps needed to achieve short-term objectives.

- Adaptive thinking
  Requires flexibility and agility to adjust strategies and approaches based on changing circumstances.

- Systematic thinking
  Involves reviewing complex situations and breaking them down into manageable systems or processes.

- Creative thinking
  Involves generating new ideas, solutions, or approaches to problems.

- Critical thinking
  Involves evaluating information, arguments, and evidence in a logical and systematic way to make the right informed decisions.

You may find yourself naturally great at some types of thinking while others are more of a challenge. Improving your thinking in those areas is one option; you could also seek support from others who excel. This could involve collaborating with someone who has complementary skills or asking yourself the right questions to elicit another perspective. The key is recognising the different thinking styles and using them effectively.

Chunking your thinking

Chunking a particular type of thinking into sustained periods rather than jumping between different types can lead to more strategic thinking. This is one of the areas covered in the time management chapter in terms of the practical aspect; however the benefit lies in chunking your thinking itself.

Jumping between different types of thinking is doable but can result in more cognitive fatigue or brain fog by the end of the day compared to spending longer periods within different thinking styles. You may also feel overwhelmed more quickly if you have a large workload and keep jumping between areas of work or required thinking.

For example, if you are working on the sales side of your business and have bits of time dotted around your week in order to get this done, you might want to have a rethink. While there is logic in ending the week with sales outreach to maintain momentum, you will gain much more from the time spent on sales when chunked into larger periods. You will notice patterns in your thinking and how to make this better in your sales process. You will also be on a 'roll' with the type of thinking required for that task, focusing on sales and action building momentum reducing the overall admin time if you were to have completed it in smaller chunks.

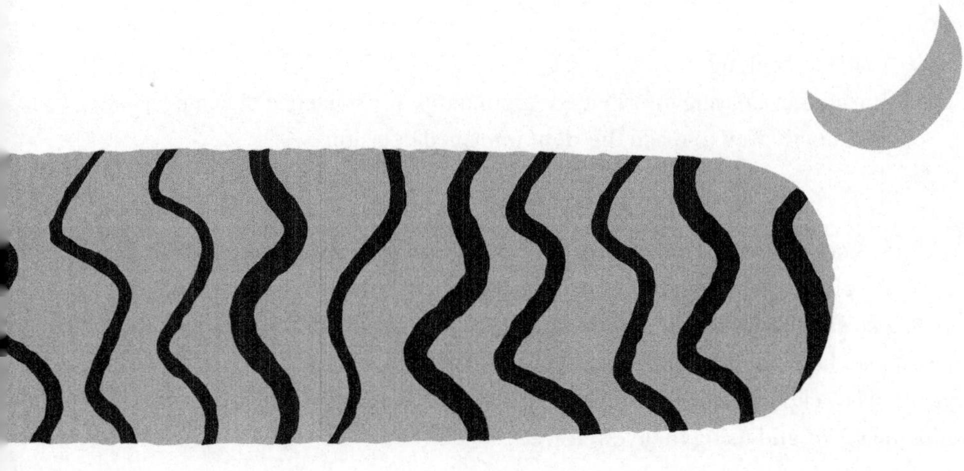

The need for quiet

Sometimes you just need quiet. To refuel and clear your mind of thoughts and regain clarity. The balance created with mental space and needed quiet time can help you sustain even the largest workloads. It enables you to find it easier to look at the bigger picture both professionally and personally, allowing yourself to have the space to see how you are feeling and to notice any thoughts you need to connect with to be on the right path for you.

In our drive for productivity and success we often overlook the importance of mental rest and reflection. Our mind requires moments of stillness to function at its best. With the constant noise that we have to put up with in our lives today, the need to balance this out with silence should be non-negotiable.

Bringing in periods of quiet reflection into our routines, taking the foot off the gas will ironically enable you to do more better. It's in these moments of reflection that we can acknowledge how we are feeling, what we are thinking, our aspirations and ensure that we are on track overall.

Self-belief

Your mindset creates your life and you can achieve anything you set out to do. However this requires belief. I'm not suggesting that absolutely everything is possible. But every great achievement stems from the unwavering self-belief of an individual, a team or a community.

If you don't believe in yourself no one else will. It's a harsh reality but it's true. You could have the best Lamborghini in a showroom, however if the salesperson is shuffling their feet and looking down when selling it, it won't get bought.

Take for instance Elon Musk, we all know who he is. He embodies unwavering self-belief. Despite facing numerous setbacks and doubts from industry experts, Musk stayed focussed in his conviction that humanity could achieve ground-breaking advancements in sustainable energy and space exploration. From financial difficulties to technical challenges, Musk continued to crack on.

His unwavering self-belief despite all this inspired thousands worldwide. But what if you don't feel that way? What if you had a tough start and how you now see yourself, either from others or your environment, tells you otherwise? Then you need to rewrite the narrative, a topic we go into further in this chapter.

Resilience

Resilience, perseverance and adaptability are what separate success from those who fall along the way. In life and career we come across inevitable challenges and setbacks that can test even the best of us. It's not just about the ability to get through tough times but using the lessons learned for growth and progress. Resilience enables us to bounce back from setbacks stronger and wiser, turning obstacles into valuable lessons. It's unwavering self-belief in our ability to reach the end goal and do whatever it takes to get there.

While resilience is about maintaining through adversity it is actually anti-fragility that shifts you over to an actual performance gain when exposed to the same scenario. Maintaining the same level of strength, however shifting the impact and the ability to instantly be able to turn any given adversity to your advantage.

Anti-fragility goes beyond robustness; basically means that you actually get stronger in the face of extreme stressors, chaos and disorder because you are facing it head on and learning rather than just 'getting through it'.

How do you develop an anti-fragile mindset?

Ultimately, developing an anti-fragile mindset is about allowing yourself to be flexible and see the learning during tough times. Here is some guidance to help you along the way:

- **Maintain a focus on learning and personal growth**
  Embrace every experience as an opportunity to learn and grow. Instead of fearing challenges, see them as chances to develop resilience and expand your toolkit.

- **Don't just be resilient, lean into the opportunity to learn**
  Resilience is crucial, but it's not just about bouncing back. It's about using setbacks as opportunities for growth, gaining valuable insights and lessons learned.

Face your fear and change your life

- **Develop the ability to flow with randomness**
  Life is unpredictable with randomness inevitable. Have the adaptability and flexibility to flow with uncertainty rather than resisting change; learn to flow with it.

- **Keep your eyes open when you're getting punched in the face**
  In moments of adversity, it's easy to become overwhelmed or lose focus. However, it's precisely during these times that opportunities often present themselves. Stay alert and open-minded, even in the face of challenges. See the learning.

- **Follow an approximate direction, not a detailed roadmap**
  While having goals and plans is essential, rigidly sticking to the roadmap can be restrictive and limiting. Instead, maintain a general direction while being open to change and unexpected opportunities along the way.

- **Staying on track**
  To enhance your mental state and create overall well-being, it's crucial to implement strategies to bring you into the right mindset at any given moment. Whether that be eliciting them or reframing to the right one.

How to improve your mental state:

- **Don't let things distract you: focus**
  We are bombarded with distractions that pull us out of the mindset we need to be in. Whether it's something else demanding our attention, the opinions of others or negativity from our own self-talk or surroundings. We must decide to take control of what we choose to focus on.

- **Rewrite the narrative**
  How we perceive things and our mindset determines our level of success in a given area. For instance, saying, "I don't have the skills I need to do this and always fail" won't put you in the right mindset. Reframe the self-talk to the opposite: "There is no reason why I can't achieve this and anything I don't know, I can figure out or learn. It is entirely possible." Shifting how you then see what you are able to achieve.

- **What is your current negative self-talk?**
  How can you rewrite it into a positive statement that reflects the opposite? Remember, this will drive you forward from where you are now, or where you see yourself, bringing you future focus and self-belief. Repeat as a mantra every time you have the negative thought come into your mind.

- **What if I just enjoyed this?**
  This is one of my favourite tools for shifting your mindset and gaining perspective. Something to use even in the most challenging of times. We so often get lost in the details or lose sight of why we are doing something, or when times get difficult, lose our way. Saying 'what if I just enjoyed this' to yourself completely challenges how you are seeing the situation around you. Give it a try.

Assessing your mindset and cognitive patterns exercise

Part 1: Evaluating your growth mindset

Take a moment to reflect on your current approach to challenges and learning experiences. Consider the following questions:

- How do you typically respond to setbacks or change to challenges?
- Are you open to learning new skills and perspectives, even if they challenge your existing beliefs?
- Do you believe that your abilities and intelligence can be developed through effort and practice?

After reflecting, write down your observations and insights about your growth mindset. Identify any areas where you may need to work on to develop a stronger growth mindset and consider what actions you can take to increase this perspective.

Part 2: *Exploring mindset states*

Think about moments in your life when you have felt completely absorbed and engaged in an activity, experiencing a sense of flow. Reflect on the following questions:

- What activities or tasks tend to bring about a state of flow for you?
- How do you feel physically, mentally, and emotionally when you are in flow?
- What factors contribute to your ability to enter a state of flow?

Once you've identified your experiences with flow, consider how you can intentionally create more opportunities to tap into this mindset in your daily life.

Part 3: *Identifying thinking patterns*

Reflect on the different types of thinking you engage in on a regular basis, such as strategic thinking, creative thinking, and critical thinking. Consider the following questions:

- In which situations do you find yourself naturally using specific types of thinking? Which situations do you struggle?
- Are there any thinking patterns that you tend to rely on more than others?
- How do your thinking patterns influence your problem-solving approach and decision-making process?

Take note of your observations and insights about your thinking patterns. Identify any areas where you may need to cultivate greater flexibility and adaptability in your thinking styles.

After completing this exercise, take some time to review your reflections and consider how you can apply the learning to enhance your mindset and cognitive abilities.

How to get your sh!t sorted

The best version of you: Mindset

- Embrace setbacks as opportunities for growth.
- Strive to achieve a state of flow in tasks and activities wherever possible.
- Expand your thinking toolkit and explore different mindset states.
- Build resilience and perseverance in the face of obstacles to maintain your focus.
- Challenge negative self-talk and reframe it with positive affirmations.
- Reflect on experiences to identify areas for mindset improvement.
- Stay open-minded and receptive to new ideas and perspectives.

Digging deeper

The best version of you: Mindset

- How do I typically respond to setbacks and challenges?
- Am I open to exploring different thinking patterns?
- Can I identify moments of flow in my daily life and how can I do this more?
- What actions can I take to nurture a growth mindset?
- What experiences have shaped my current mindset and do I need to reframe any of my thinking or self-talk?

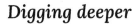

Notes, musings and thoughts to myself

(Use these pages to make notes on what you've read to help get your sh!t together)

There is beauty in the darkest moments.

If you find it then you have truly learned.

CHAPTER 4

The best version of you: Energy

CHAPTER 4

ENERGY

In this chapter, we explore the key aspect of energy management and its impact on our daily lives. We discuss energy renewal and depletion zones, highlighting how they influence our interactions and outcomes.

By practising mindfulness and being self-aware, we can smartly use these zones effectively creating the right energy states. The chapter highlights the importance of managing energy levels for productivity and well-being, and creating environments for positive energy flow.

What if you just decided to ENJOY EVERYTHING today?

The type of energy you use day-to-day

We are using energy even when we think we aren't. It's a constant flow of energy use. Replacing what we've used with the right food and adequate rest ensures we put it back to a certain extent.

Issues arise when we function in above-average daily energy levels of output. For example, athletes or high performers need to match their diet to support them and be more mindful of what they are eating to support them. To refuel.

Mental focus requires much more energy than we give it credit for. In fact, a very successful acupuncturist once said to me that when we are stressed, our mind can feel like it has run a whole marathon in terms of energy output. However, it's an area in the Western world that doesn't get much air time.

An entrepreneurs journey

I've worked with hundreds of entrepreneurs and peak performers over the years and their journey can be both exhilarating and challenging. As they work through the inevitable ups and downs of building their business they often face various obstacles that impact their energy levels and overall well-being.

When working at such a level and pace, it's common to feel overwhelmed by the demands of running a business. Long hours, tight timelines and constant pressure can have a big impact on their physical and mental health. To maintain the right energy levels and sustain productivity we need to look after ourselves and be on top of our well-being. As I've already highlighted, this includes taking regular breaks, working out or at least bringing movement into our day and practising mindfulness techniques to reduce stress and promote mental clarity.

Managing energy effectively is essential for long-term success. By listening to our bodies, we can recognise signs of burnout and take proactive steps to 'fill back up'. Ultimately, finding a balance between work and personal life is key to sustaining energy levels and achieving success.

Energy: renewal and depletion zones

We swing between energy states that can either easily be maintained and fill us up or the opposite that deplete us. Known as energy renewal and depletion zones, these different states of energy are experienced throughout the day.

Functioning in the renewal zone, we feel energised, focused and motivated with a strong ability to be productive and tackle tasks efficiently. On the other hand, functioning in the depletion zone can quickly bring on fatigue, low motivation and decreased productivity.

Understanding these energy zones helps us manage our energy levels more effectively by checking at any given moment as to which side we are functioning on.

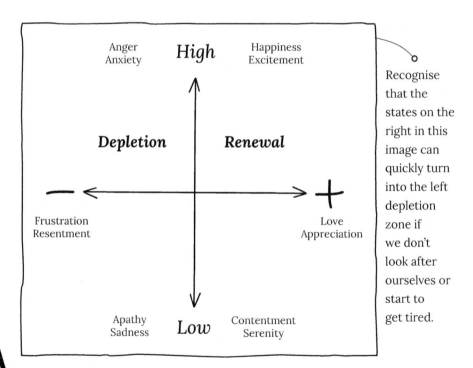

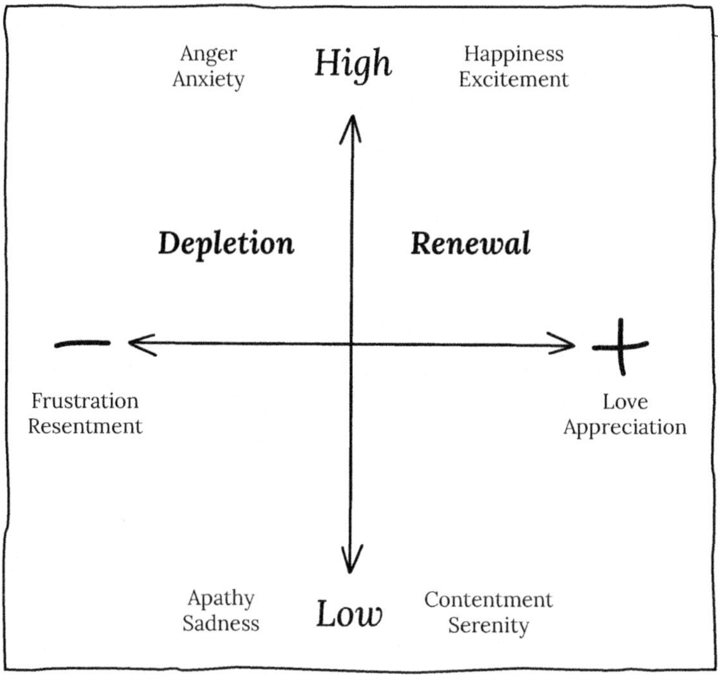

Recognise that the states on the right in this image can quickly turn into the left depletion zone if we don't look after ourselves or start to get tired.

You can use the strategies outlined in the next section 'From Survival to Thrive' to counter this and to ensure that you stay in the renewal zone.

Survival energy state

There are energy states that we are able to maintain easily and other states that will pretty much burn us out at high speed. For anyone who has either experienced trauma in their past, has struggled or finds themselves performing in a role or area that they are not comfortable with, they can very easily shift into 'survival energy'.

Functioning in a survival energy state is just not sustainable because it keeps the individual in a constant state of stress and hyperarousal. In survival mode, the body and mind perceive threats everywhere, leading to heightened levels of anxiety, fear and stress. When functioning in survival energy the body's resources are primarily directed towards immediate survival responses such as fight, flight or freeze.

This moves energy away from essential functions like digestion, immune response and cognitive processing. Which are necessary for long-term health and well-being. Leading to common stress symptoms like IBS and other illnesses so common today. Prolonged exposure to survival energy can lead to physical and mental health issues such as chronic fatigue, digestive problems, anxiety disorders and burnout. It massively depletes decision-making abilities, reduces creativity and productivity and overall quality of life.

I myself spent many of my earlier years functioning in this state due to a stressful childhood and the need to survive on my own for a while when I was younger. What I did learn is that when I shifted the state from 'survival' to 'thrive' I could not only enjoy more of what I was doing, it was maintainable for sustained periods and meant that the ceiling was completely lifted in what I was able to achieve.

Thrive energy state

Thrive energy is a much more positive and sustainable energy type, leading to peak well-being and performance. Where individuals feel a deep sense of vitality, clarity and purpose. It is more than just physical energy; it is a total alignment of mind, body and spirit that enables us to meet challenges with resilience and the right mindset.

In the thrive energy state you experience a sense of vitality and aliveness, ready to take on whatever challenges and opportunities come your way. This energy state helps us maintain a positive outlook on life, approaching each day with a sense of optimism and possibility. With the ability to remain calm and composed and the ability to bounce back quickly.

Thriving individuals have a clear understanding of what matters most to them in life and they ensure that their actions and decisions align. This provides them with a strong sense of meaning and fulfilment, feeding their motivation and drive.

From Survival to Thrive Mode

So how do you shift your energy state? There are practical areas that you could work on around your situation combined with these practical tips to go from survival to thrive mode:

- Spot triggers
  Identify situations, people or environments that cause stress or anxiety for you. Take steps to address and manage them.

- Get mindful
  Bring mindfulness techniques like meditation, deep breathing or yoga into your day. Take time to slow down and connect your thoughts and emotions. Take a walk in nature. Holistic therapies such as acupuncture have also been a tool that I swear by to maintain all that I do. Self-care, self-care, self-care.

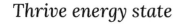

- **Create boundaries**
  Stop saying yes all the time if you do. Say no to taking on extra tasks or projects that overwhelm you. Focus on spending your time in areas that you need to get done or fill you up. Selfish or is it?

- **Challenge limiting beliefs**
  Reduce negative self-talk and beliefs that slow you down. Replace them with powerful empowering thoughts, recognise how great you are and all that you do well. Focus on this to lift yourself up into the right state.

The energy you give out

The energy you give out plays a significant role in shaping your relationships and circumstances. It's often said that you get back what you give out, with how you show up influencing your experiences and interactions. Consistently displaying positivity and openness tends to elicit similar responses from others and creates opportunities for positive interactions and growth.

Your attitude, presence and emotional state contribute to the energy you project. This influences both personal and professional relationships and quite frankly opportunities. Being fully aware of the energy you give out at any given moment is essential for becoming the best version of yourself.

Imagine the potential for creation and achievement if you cultivate awareness in this area. I challenge you to dedicate a day to improving and monitoring your interactions with others. Show more interest, smile more, or listen more. Notice how this shift attracts more opportunities and positive responses. Now consider implementing this practice every day.

Chaos and
challenge
kick in just
before the
breakthrough.
Don't give up

How to get your sh!t sorted

The best version of you: Energy

- Recognise the importance of managing energy levels for productivity and well-being.
- Understand the impact of different energy states on personal and professional interactions.
- Be mindful of the energy you project and how it influences your relationships.
- Bring in mindfulness practices to maintain the right energy levels throughout the day.
- Practice self-awareness to identify and address situations that may deplete your energy.
- Create an environment that encourages positive energy for yourself and others.

Digging deeper

The best version of you: Energy

- Reflect on situations where I have felt energised and motivated versus times when I have felt depleted and fatigued. What factors contributed to these different energy states?

- Consider the people I interact with regularly. How does their energy affect my own and how do I influence theirs?

- What strategies or techniques from this chapter could I bring into my daily routine to maintain the right energy levels?

- How can I become more mindful of the energy I project? What do I need to change?

- Think about a recent experience where I consciously shifted from a depletion zone to a renewal zone. What actions did I take and what was the outcome?

- In what ways can I create an environment that nurtures positive energy for myself and those around me? Have I even thought about that before?

Notes, musings and thoughts to myself

(Use these pages to make notes on what you've read to help get your sh!t together)

CHAPTER 5
Habits

CHAPTER 5
HABITS

In the habits chapter, we explore the power of consistency and commitment in shaping our daily routines. By adopting the CARE approach; Consistent Action, Adopting a Better Mindset, Reinforcing Self-Belief and Embracing Commitment. We establish a framework for sustaining positive habits and look at aligning our habits with our end goal of being the best version of ourselves. Essentially learning to create a habit routine that encourages growth and well-being.

A habit is when you have done something so many times that your body lets your response kick in automatically without thinking about it. For example, waking up in the morning, people often begin to think about what isn't working and they feel sad or not happy. It's automatic.

Various research suggests that it takes around on average 66 days to change a habit. Now for some this can be much less, some as little as 18 days. On the other side of the spectrum are those that need a very large amount of time, as much as 250 days, right through to those who really struggle to maintain any habits or routines at all.

The 21/90 rule reinforces the thinking that it takes 21 days to make a habit and 90 days to make it a permanent lifestyle change. So if you can make it to 21 days and continue, you've made a longer term change.

Sometimes you
have to *let go*
of something
that matters

to create
space

woah, look at
this space

for something
better.

Habits are energy savers

We stack habits as part of growing and developing and being able to function in the world. From our earliest days we are remembering and programming our minds to carry those on. From the day-to-day to how we react to our environment. So it makes sense that we have them on autopilot rather than needing to actively think about what we are seeing and our reaction to it.

If we didn't have habits, we would never get anything done. That autopilot setting is fundamental for our day-to-day functioning. What this means is that we conserve a huge amount of energy not having to refigure things out and are able to survive.

You don't forget habits

Regardless of the amount of time since you have changed a habit, which can be even a year or so, it does not mean that you have completely forgotten about it. Ultimately, we never forget our habits. This way if a scenario we manage to get through occurs again, ideally, we can pull the habits to survive out of our memory and put them into action.

This doesn't mean that every habit has served us. For example, when things go wrong, we may turn to a particular way of dealing with them throughout our lives unless we actively look to remove the bad habit and replace it with another.

Up to 40% of what you do is habitual

The majority of people have up to 45% of the action that they take on a day-to-day basis the same as before which means that much time is on autopilot.

The logic being that we are then free to be able to spend the rest of the time working and functioning in more of an agile way taking in the information around us and analysing it accordingly. We can create daily habits that help us perform better, for example, a number of entrepreneurs chose to wear the same items of clothing each day to reduce wasted time on deciding this such as Steve Jobs and Barack Obama.

Your past goals are found in your habits

As said earlier our habits are with us for life whether in use or not. They started by doing something enough times that it stuck. Quite commonly we adjust our habits to attain a new goal or attainment that we need in order to accomplish it.

Habits that we may have started when we were younger that would help us to be able to hang out with the cool crowd for example, were appropriate for the time but ones to move forward from. Our habits stay in the back of our mind as in previous programs, our mind doesn't know that we have moved on, just that this is a habit that no longer serves us but is remembered deep in the back of our subconscious mind.

Habits that will keep you on track

As said earlier our habits are with us for life whether in use or not. They started by doing something enough times that it stuck. Quite commonly we adjust our habits to attain a new goal or attainment that we need in order to accomplish it.

Habits for personal well-being

- Physical exercise & movement
  Regular physical activity for health and vitality, which is part of the three key aspects.

- The right diet for you
  Again another part of the physical aspect in our foundations. Nourishing your body with the right foods ensures sustained energy and wellness.

- Mindset
  Being aware of your mindset and in the present to gain maximum impact at any given moment, reducing stress and enhancing mental clarity and opportunity to grow.

- Relaxation
  Re-centre with time to unwind, these practices will rejuvenate your mind and body.

- Self-awareness and authenticity
  Exploring personal dynamics and aligning actions with core values making sure that you are on the right track. For you.

Habits for personal well-being

- Hobbies
  Time in activities outside work that help you to feel grounded and that you enjoy.

- Family and relationships
  Ensuring you find time for meaningful connections enhancing emotional well-being.

- Health and fitness
  Here it is again, a fundamental aspect right at the core of who you are.

- Career / work
  Doing what you love and are good at. Striving for continuous growth and fulfilment.

- Financial management
  Being on top of your finances and planning to bring stability to all areas of your life.

- Spiritual exploration and reflection
  Seeking meaning and purpose, ultimately we are all looking for the meaning of life.

Empowering habits

- Power-boosting activities
  Activities that boost motivation and enthusiasm.

- Growth practices
  Setting and achieving meaningful objectives drives growth.

- Progress-driven routines
  Consistent habits that move you forwards for personal growth and development.

- Make it enjoyable
  Having daily routines that you actually enjoy increases the chance of you continuing them. And if you don't ask, "What if I just enjoyed this?"

- Daily review
  Recognise what you have achieved each day to gear your mindset for continued success the next day.

Career and business-boosting habits

- Work on the important stuff
  Focusing on high-impact important tasks at any given time maximises productivity and efficiency.

- Strategic planning
  Clear objectives and action plans drive growth. Full stop.

- Performance and evaluation
  Regular review and adjustment of strategies ensure continuous improvement.

Your habits for success

What if you were the best version of yourself? Your best version of yourself are all the habits and times you have been doing well mixed together. Often people can only manage to maintain up to two good habits at any one time and flit between this throughout the year.

You at your very top, the very best of your game are all of these habits at the same time. The reason this is rare is that the majority of people aren't actively making a habit of lifestyle changes and don't have the tools to sustain them and so they then drop off.

Defining your best habits

In order to review and define the best habits for you,
here are some key questions:

- Who do you want to be?
- What habits would make that a success?
- List the habits you want to change
- List the habits you would like to keep
- What new habits serve you?
- What did you do before that worked when maintaining a habit?

We all have muscle and mind memory, so we are all capable of eliciting the right habits and keeping them all at once. Admittedly it does take focus and an understanding of how we can remove, keep and gain new habits.

Starting and keeping new habits

When it comes to new habits and sticking with them, it's important to approach the process with intention and practical strategies. Here are some tips to help you integrate and maintain new habits effectively:

- Focus on one habit at a time
  Instead of overwhelming yourself with multiple changes, start by focusing on one habit until it becomes part of your routine. Once you've mastered one habit, you can gradually introduce others.

- Stack your habits
  Pairing new habits with existing ones can help reinforce the behaviour and remind you to do them. By linking a new habit to something you already do regularly, you create a natural trigger that reminds you to follow through.

- Use reminders
  Use reminders such as post-it notes or digital alerts to keep you accountable and on track with your new habit. These visual cues serve as gentle reminders of your commitment.

- Link challenging habits with enjoyable ones
  If you find a particular habit challenging or less enjoyable, try connecting it with something you do enjoy doing either before or after. This positive association can make the habit more appealing and increase your motivation to stick with it.

- Reward yourself
  Recognise your efforts and progress by rewarding yourself along the way. Celebrate small victories and milestones as you work towards integrating the new habit into your lifestyle. Remember, self-improvement should feel rewarding, not like a punishment!

- Notice the impact
  Take note of the positive changes and benefits that come from implementing your new habit. Noting the impact of your efforts reinforces your commitment and encourages continued growth and development.

Losing Bad Habits

When it comes to getting rid of bad habits, it's important to approach the process with honesty and commitment. Here are some steps to help you identify and replace negative habits effectively. You might want to write each of these down, taking time to reflect on each stage.

Stage 1 - Recognise the negative habits
Some habits no longer align with the person you want to be or are actually moving you backwards or working against what you are looking to do. Take the time to note which habits these are and decide that they no longer serve you.

Stage 2 - Reflect on the motivation for change
Understand why you want to break free from these habits. Define your motivations clearly to stay focused and committed to the process of replacing negative habits with positive ones. What are these and how will you make sure that these are your go to moving forwards?

Stage 3 - Review and replace
Once you've identified unsupportive habits and clarified your motivations, take proactive steps to replace them with positive alternatives. Choose new habits that align with your goals and values, ensuring they contribute to your personal growth and well-being.

If you want to change or remove habits, you have to be massively committed to getting rid of them. Remind yourself why you are doing this and the overall impact that this will have to keep you on track. Reward yourself and recognise the changes that you are making successfully, daily. Remember we only have one life so it is up to you how you live it.

CARE *for your habits*

By following the CARE approach you create a supportive framework for sustaining your best habits, ensuring you stay as the best version of yourself.

This requires:

Consistent Action

Adopting a Better Mindset

Reinforcing Self-Belief

Embracing Commitment

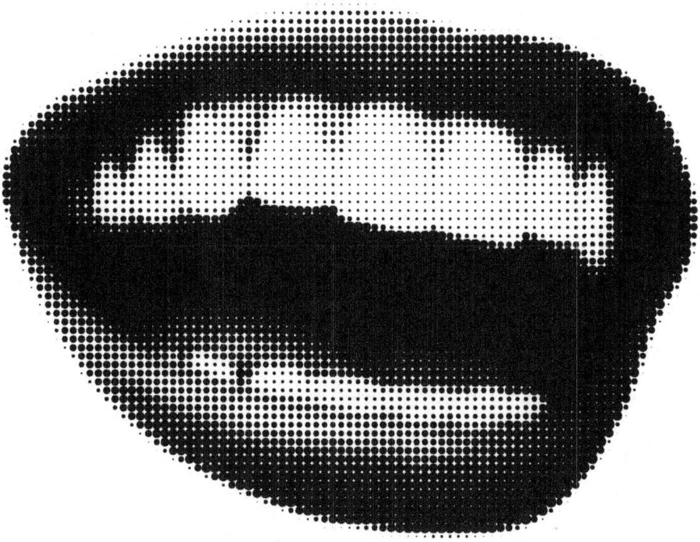

Consistent action

The key to maintaining positive habits lies in consistency. Understand that it's okay to mess up occasionally; what really counts is your overall dedication and persistence. Let consistent action be your guide.

Adopting a better mindset

Every journey towards maintaining great habits starts with the mindset. Shift your thinking towards growth and improvement. By deciding to be better every day, you upgrade your mindset and open yourself to new possibilities.

Reinforcing self-belief

Believing in yourself is a non-negotiable. Completely believe in your ability to maintain your habits and make positive long-term changes. Maintain your determination and get through most obstacles that come your way.

Embracing commitment

Commitment is the core of maintaining any habit at all. Taking your commitment seriously means being dedicated to your habits, even when challenged. Remind yourself why you started and the benefits these habits bring to your life. Stay end goal focused.

How to get your sh!t sorted

The best version of you: Habits

- Recognise that occasional setbacks are just part of the process, just maintain consistency regardless.

- Surround yourself with the right support who can offer encouragement and reinforce your positive habits.

- Keep on top of your progress and adjust your approach if needed to remain on track with your objectives.

- Create an awareness around your self-care and well-being to sustain the energy and motivation required for habit maintenance.

- Recognise the importance of consistently taking action to sustain positive habits.

- Develop a strong sense of self-belief in your ability to maintain habits and effect long-term positive change.

Digging deeper

The best version of you: Habits

- What new habit could I start today that will have the biggest impact on my personal and professional growth?

- How do my current habits support me to be the person I want to be?

- What is one habit I could stop today that would have the most positive impact on my life?

- How can I apply the CARE approach to ensure the sustainability of my new habits?

- What challenges do I anticipate in maintaining my new habits, and how can I plan to overcome them?

- How will changing my mindset to one of growth and improvement affect my journey towards better habits?

- What commitment am I willing to make to myself to ensure I follow through with these changes?

- Who in my life can support me in this journey and how can I engage them?

Notes, musings and thoughts to myself

(Use these pages to make notes on what you've read to help get your sh!t together)

CHAPTER 6
Actions

CHAPTER 6

ACTIONS

In the Actions chapter, we look at the importance of aligning actions further with long-term goals and values. Through practical tools and insightful advice, showing how to assess the quality and impact of actions on personal and professional growth. Focusing on the need for awareness of the actions that you take, the chapter encourages continuous reflection and adjustment to ensure actions remain in sync with priorities and as such growth.

The actions that we take not only maintain but also shape our present and future lives. Each choice, each action, each deliberate step forwards, creates either a positive or negative outcome. The connection between choice, action and outcome cannot be overstated. It's a continuous cycle where decisions and actions shape the results we experience in both life and business. The key lies in the choice.

SITUATION >> CHOICE 1 >> ACTION >> OUTCOME

SITUATION >> CHOICE 2 >> ACTION >> OUTCOME

What we do need to remind ourselves is that we are actually in complete control of the actions that we do decide to take. That to create an awareness at the point of choice is the game changer.

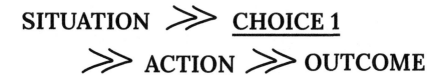

There is no point managing your time well if you spend it on *the wrong things*

The right type of actions

Being action orientated, taking the steps needed to ensure that you are constantly moving forwards is another big driver for success. However as we all know a high percentage of the time can be spent on tasks and actions that take us in the opposite direction.

You should at any time be aware what type of action you are taking and whether it moves you forwards or in fact takes you backwards. Aligned actions. Once you start to take control and measure this, then you really start to see progress improvements and more of an awareness and smart use of your time.

Aligned actions

What we are able to achieve is all about the quality of the actions that we are taking. These need to be truly in line with several areas to make them aligned, our why or our business why, what we need to do to achieve that and when.

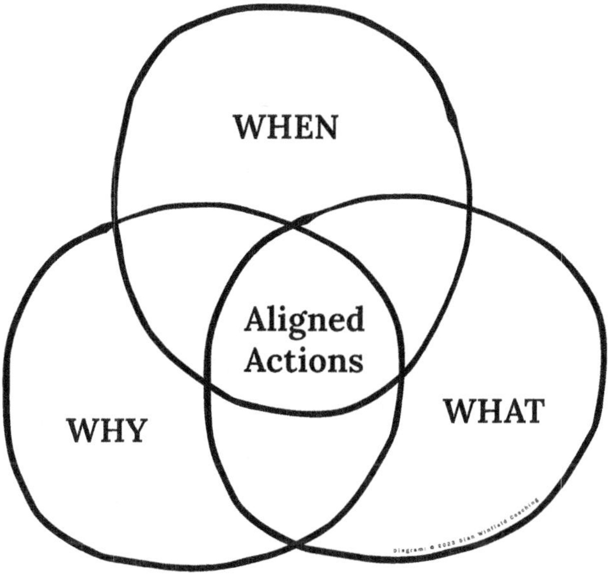

Aligned actions = maximum productivity

WHY

One of the fundamentals for ensuring that you are in the right place and that you are working or pushing forward in the right area is whether or not what you are doing aligns with your values and what matters to you.

- Do you really care about the work that you do?
- Are you motivated by the impact that it has?

A great example of the importance of this is when starting or growing a company. It takes grit and determination to start or scale a company. You and your whole team need to be completely committed and understand your WHY. This will keep you all pushing through the more challenging times.

The same goes for you individually. In order to be fulfilled we must be motivated by what we do and see it as bigger than ourselves. This gives us that extra energy to see hard times through and be motivated when others may struggle.

WHAT

What you do comes in a few forms.
Firstly you need do ***the right type of work***:

- Working in the right industry
- The right job or starting / building the right type of business for you
- The right type of work: hands on or leadership
- That the company is the right culture fit for you or that you create the right culture
- That you can work with those around you

If any of the above aren't in tune with you, then again motivation will be negatively impacted. It is easy to find yourself late in your career having amassed a great deal of experience but not completely happy with what you are doing. This is because subconsciously you know that you are now in the position to be able to now tweak the work that you do to better suit your experience and you.

Secondly, it is ***the work itself***. You need to be extremely clear on the work and tasks that you need to do in order to achieve what you set out to do and the time management piece is the 'getting it done'.

This is a lengthy piece to cover off however, you need to be clear that the tasks and the work that you are doing are in line with these key areas:

- The overall strategy (business or personal)
- Your individual role or responsibilities
- Your business and personal growth

If this is the case, then as is shown in the Aligned Actions Matrix diagram, you will be taking aligned actions leading to maximum productivity.

WHEN

The final piece to consider in this matrix is the ***when***. As well as it being in line with the key areas above, you can ultimately only do one thing at a time yourself so understanding what you need to do well is the art behind getting these all done. The first thing to consider is the overall timelines for projects or strategic objectives.

It is key to have a clear idea of when these are due for delivery. It works to have something centrally located to track these and to bring these into your task planning.

The second is when looking at everything that you need to do as a whole. Understanding what your priorities truly are will help you define the order of selection when faced with multiple tasks to do and to get the order within which you do these correctly. So if you are clear that your priorities are, for example, top level projects for your clients, bringing money in or staying on top of managing your team, then other tasks will take second place to this and not disturb the priority tasks you need to zero in on.

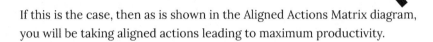

The 80:20 rule of workload can be great to follow to keep on track. This means that 20 percent of our work contributes less than 80 percent of its value, so focus on the most important 20 per cent in order to complete the most crucial tasks.

This will increase your performance at work so the key tasks or projects are complete. This way you are also likely to be less frazzled when a random less important task hits your desk.

When each of these areas in the above section have been considered, these then become aligned actions specific to you, maximising productivity. As with anything, these will change so reviewing periodically is a good idea, I suggest yearly or bi-yearly which we go in to in chapter 10.

Action direction assessment (ASR *actions*)

So how do we make sure that more often than not, you are taking yourself in the right direction, to growth. We need to measure whether the actions you are taking overall daily are moving you forwards, keeping you on the spot, or in fact taking you backwards.

Below is a simple tool to help keep in mind at any given moment what type of action you are taking and the quality of it based on what your priorities are. I've found this a complete game changer. Creating an awareness of the actions you are taking are moving you forwards 'Advancing', keeping you in the same place 'Static' or taking you backwards 'Regressive'.

You will need to be clear on your overall objectives and goals and what you should be doing to achieve these. Interestingly, most people don't align their day to day actions with these and get lost in just doing random tasks that they think are driving growth. You should at any given moment know the 3-4 tasks or actions to take that will be most valuable to you. Finding yourself in this space, this really is the best version of yourself.

You can track the actions daily if you like or you can just reflect at the end of each day and bullet point the main actions you have taken and decide where they sit. After a while you will naturally pick advancing actions more and where needed reduce down or field out the static ones and have reduced the time spent in regressing ones without the need to track.

Advancing actions

These actions will take you forward and are completely in line with not only your priorities but all that you are looking to achieve. They also should be in line with your values and when you are doing these tasks you know you are making progress.

At a minimum, you need to have one task that does this completed a day, however if you want to have major progress forwards, the majority of the actions you take need to sit in this lane, with the other actions either someone else picking up, being automated or in chunks of time with minimal impact on growth.

Questions to ask when looking to assess your actions:

- By doing this am I moving forwards, standing still or going backwards?
- Is this task aligned with what I should be working on?
- Is this taking me forwards creating momentum with this or creating something? If yes to the last two then you are contributing to your progress and growth. They will advance you in the right direction creating momentum and driving you to where you want to be.

Static actions

These actions are required, however, they will keep you in the same place essentially. Vanilla tasks I call them. This includes project management around what you are doing, admin, keeping on top of messages emails or communications. For those that need to have meetings and calls with others, then you can also review whether that use of your time will be useful and is an advancing action, or that perhaps it could be shorter, a zoom, an email or someone else could pick It up. Everything you do is linked to a choice and an action.

Questions to ask when looking to assess your actions:

- By doing this am I moving forwards, standing still or going backwards?
- Is this task necessary for what I need to work on?
- Could I spend less time on it or could someone else pick it up or automate?
- Are my actions too 'static' or 'regressive' today? Does it have to be done today and can I replace it with an action that drives forwards?

Regressive actions

These take away from your progress, like wasting time or procrastinating, even though these don't seem an action, it is a choice and you are choosing to take no action. Perfectionism will also lead you to find yourself in this area, with spending too much time on checking or fine-tuning and not enough on getting the right things done.

Lack of clarity on your overall goals and objectives can also mean that the quality of your actions will sit in this zone. Random things you are getting done of no real value. And finally actions that destroy or self-sabotage that completely counter your progress. Some of these include overspending, tipping the balance in drinking or other areas that don't support you moving forwards and are in fact taking you back.

Questions to ask when looking to assess your actions:

- By doing this am I moving forwards, standing still or going backwards?
- Why am I doing this?
- How important is progress and what I am looking to achieve to me?
- What could I be doing instead that will take me forwards?

Defining your 'Advancing', 'Static' or 'Regressive' actions

For those who want to delve deeper into understanding which actions fall on the above scale, on the next page I have created an exercise to support this. This can be used as a way to determine where your actions sit. Place them in the top half if they contribute to moving you forward, in the middle if they are maintaining your current position and at the bottom for those that are pushing you backwards.

For example, at the bottom is 'Procrastinating or delaying important tasks or deadlines,' both a time drain and something that sets you back. This may seem obvious, and what we aim to do here is create awareness around the less obvious to prompt recognition and subsequently, change.

> ***Everything*** you do is linked to a ***choice*** and an ***action.***

ASR Action Scale

+	Networking that increases professional connections.	Advancing
	Time on routine administrative tasks.	Static
–	Procrastinating or delaying important tasks or deadlines.	Regressive

Here are some other examples of actions that sit in each area to get you started

Advancing actions

- Actions that help towards the completion of significant projects or tasks.
- Seeking out learning opportunities through online courses or industry webinars.
- Networking that increases professional connections.
- Time in personal development activities like reading or listening to podcasts.
- Time to innovate processes to improve team efficiency.

Static actions

- Time on routine administrative tasks.
- Maintain existing skills without seeking new challenges.
- Resist change or new technologies that could enhance productivity.
- The same routine without exploring alternatives.
- Interactions within existing networks.

Regressive actions

- Procrastinating or delaying important tasks or deadlines.
- Engaging in negative self-talk or limiting beliefs.
- Allowing fear of failure to prevent exploration of new ideas.
- Dwelling on past mistakes instead of focusing on lessons learned.
- Engaging in distracting activities that hinder professional or personal goals.

Your action filter

Most of us don't think to the extent of what we are doing and how we take action. However, another fundamental to the right action is the realisation that we all have filters or maps of the world and an opinion of it and ourselves. This shapes our choices and subsequently what we choose to do. Our ability to grow. Here are a few questions to ask yourself to think about this further:

- Is my current view of myself, who I am and my capabilities as good as they should be? If not, how can I improve this?

- Is my current understanding or view of my role and my ability to perform well impacted by how I see myself or other people?

- When was the last time I sat down and thought about how I view the world and others around me? How does that impact my actions and ability to grow?

These are quite big questions and may take a while to answer. Grab a pad and pen or use the space at the end of this chapter and spend some time on them to see the real value of this exercise. Then consider what changes you need to make.

Stop
wasting
time carrying
other people.
You only have
one life.

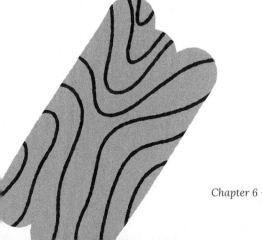

How to get your sh!t sorted

The best version of you: Actions

- Regularly review whether your actions are aligned with your goals and values.
- Prioritise tasks that contribute to your personal and professional growth.
- Be mindful of the quality of your actions and their impact on your progress.
- Strive to increase advancing actions while minimising static and regressive ones.
- Maintain awareness of how your actions influence your overall well-being and productivity.
- Continuously refine your approach to ensure that your actions lead you closer to your desired outcomes.

Digging deeper

The best version of you: Actions

- Are my daily actions in line with my main goals, driving me forward and not holding me back?
- How well am I prioritising tasks to focus on what truly matters for my growth?
- How many of your current actions sit within the 'advancing' action zone compared to the 'static' or 'regressing' actions? What did I take away from that section?
- What steps can I take to improve the quality of my actions overall?
- Am I aware of how my actions affect my well-being and productivity?
- How can I strengthen the connection between my daily actions and my long-term goals?

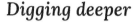

Notes, musings and thoughts to myself

(Use these pages to make notes on what you've read to help get your sh!t together)

CHAPTER 7
Knowing who you are

CHAPTER 7

KNOWING WHO YOU ARE

In the chapter "Knowing Who You Are," we discuss the importance of self-awareness and authenticity for personal growth and development. Through anecdotes and reflections, highlighting the benefit of embracing authenticity and self-acceptance. Exploring personality tests like Myers Briggs, Caliper Profile, and DISC Profile, the chapter offers practical tools for self-discovery, enabling deeper insights into how to become more aware and as such the best version of yourself.

Knowing yourself and being authentic is key to your overall performance. As we mentioned in the action chapter, you are the filter within which you see the world. So in this instance how you perform is the tool within which things get done. Interestingly, I was torn between having this chapter here or before actions (with 'knowing who you are' the filter) however, I have chosen for this to sit here. It makes sense that there is true power in understanding who you are and how you actually function. Showing up authentically regardless of what people think and really tapping in to the best version of yourself.

Growing as an individual can only be done when we allow vulnerability. Are open to look at ourselves at the core of our weaknesses and areas we could work on. Just leaning in to what you are good at will give you off-balance progress and just as they say with actions, it's not the things you do but the things you don't do that have the biggest impact.

We tend to do what is easier, it is easier to continue to get stronger in the areas we thrive in. However true growth and progression comes from building up our weaknesses and getting better in those areas. As with any areas that we don't pay attention to, sooner or later the parts you are not looking at will build up into something that exists as a problem or a set-back. If you were addressing all areas from the outset, the problem wouldn't exist at all.

Be **true** and **authentic** with your **decisions** and you will **always** be on

the right path

Authenticity

It seems fitting that I share an authentic story here in this section of the book, taking a moment to share my own journey with authenticity and the value of it.

It wasn't until I showed up authentically as myself that true personal growth and success happened. Until then, I felt as if I was playing a game, not always happy with what I was saying or the results that I was getting but felt that I was doing what everyone else did. Perhaps emulating or learning from peers or people I admired too closely, yet to find my own path there. Now building a business and helping other people has always come easily to me, however, as you will be aware, it is one thing being an expert for others, another for yourself.

We are bombarded with messages over social media and in the books we read about when we should get up, how much we should read, what podcasts to listen to, what we should eat. I, like anyone else, completely understand the value of a growth mindset, and in fact, think that it is fundamental to be able to create the world that you want as I outline in this book but sometimes it all feels like forced fun.

For me, in the very early days, I felt that there was almost an unspoken expectation to follow the conveyor belt view of what being an entrepreneur meant and therefore creating validation for being in that space. Write a book, create a podcast, say smart stuff, say smart relevant things on the topic. Keep up to date with your hashtags, create cool videos, the same as everyone else but just slightly unique so you stand out, but not too far away.

How authentic during this process are we being? Or are we just following a crowd like being in with the 'cool kids' at school?

Some time ago, I had quite an exciting opportunity to be able to speak to an all-female audience in a globally established company ahead of me. As the date of the event loomed rather than feeling excited, I started to feel a sense of heaviness, of not wanting to take part. As the date grew closer I continued to feel off, this was a great opportunity why was I feeling this way?
A few days before the event, I found myself in front of my wardrobe with the

doors wide open looking at the assortment of funky tops, t-shirts, trousers, jeans, and flat slip-on shoes and Converse. I don't have anything to wear. Where did I put those heels I had? Where were those dresses? I probably need to get my hair done. Everyone else does.

At the same time, I had dug out my bio to be able to reel this off at the beginning of the panel. Odd that we do that. We know who we are and yet we need to rehearse to say it in exactly the right way and to start with what we have accomplished or our academic achievements. Again it all felt off.

It was a few months before this that I had found myself on another panel. It was about starting a business and the advice around it. I found myself giving advice around the questions we were asked and status quo style answers around strategy or business plans.

Now I have worked with hundreds of start-ups and have over 25 years of experience behind me, so I can easily reel off this stuff. But looking back I realise that I was just playing the game. I had some much more to say on what the journey really entails, the ways around the status quo that we are presented with to make something happen, the sheer grit needed. Holding back my desire to yawn when we started talking in the usual expected way about the investment space and how to secure it, I left the panel feeling like I had made myself be quiet to fit in.

So it was the day before the global panel event. That morning I found myself typing an email to the organisers taking myself off the panel and of course profusely apologised. I had never or would never normally do this, so why now? Conforming. Being someone that I wasn't.

Why was I feeling the need to dress and show up like all the other panellists when that wasn't me? Why do I need to highlight academic achievements in an almost competitive way with my co-panellists rather than embracing each of our individuality and the core grit of achievement however success has been achieved?

I had feedback in my very early days from a peer about the clothes that I should wear for a photo shoot. I wanted to wear jeans, a t-shirt, chunky chain, smart jacket, and trainers. To show up like I would normally. I was told you shouldn't wear jeans, you need to dress in more formal clothes for others to take you seriously in business. Why?

On reflection after this point, I have more often than not seen my male counterparts show up in jeans and a shirt even down to this being acceptable for Steve Jobs and look what he achieved. Was he told he should dress smarter for a shoot?

It has taken some time on my own journey to give myself permission to show up as myself, to now lean into who I am and be ok with that rather than just blindly agree with the status quo that we are being presented with. And as soon as I did that the ceiling rose, in fact, I really don't think that there is any ceiling at all now.

> I had never or would never normally do this, ***so why now?*** ***Conforming.*** Being someone that I wasn't.

Personality tests

Now let's be clear, there is not right or wrong, good or bad measurement or judging with a personality. The idea here is just to advise that you look under the bonnet to see who you truly are and that this has a huge impact on your ability to be the best version of yourself.

There are many of these personality tests available, each with their own value and tried and tested methods for bringing you or a company clarity on an individual or team and how they function. Here are a few of the main ones as examples:

Myers Briggs

The Myers Briggs Type Indicator (MBTI) was created by Isabel Briggs Myers and her mother Katharine Cook Briggs and is based on Carl Jung's personality type theory. It's a widely used psychometric assessment tool in the workplace designed to assess individual preferences across four areas: Extraversion (E) vs. Introversion (I), Sensing (S) vs. Intuition (N), Thinking (T) vs. Feeling (F), and Judging (J) vs. Perceiving (P). The MBTI highlights within which one of 16 personality types, such as ISTJ, ENFP, etc., each individual sits and provides insights into aspects of their personality and behaviour.

The MBTI helps individuals gain a deeper understanding of their preferences, decision-making processes, and communication styles. By identifying their strengths, weaknesses, and potential areas for growth, they can make more informed career choices along with the ability to interact with others more effectively. For companies, the MBTI focuses on team building, conflict resolution and leadership development by creating better communication and collaboration among team members and in the workplace.

Caliper profile

Created by Herb Greenberg and Albert S. Tannenbaum in 1961, the Caliper Profile is a psychometric assessment tool used for team member selection, recruitment management, and leadership development. It evaluates personality traits, motivations, and potential performance in various job roles. Unlike other personality tests, the Caliper Profile focuses on identifying individuals' unique strengths and areas for development, providing companies with valuable insights into potential candidates' fit within the workplace.

Companies benefit from the Caliper Profile by making more informed recruitment decisions, identifying high-potential employees, and creating specific development plans in line with individual strengths and developmental needs. By aligning the team's skills with job roles and company objectives, the Caliper Profile enhances employee engagement, retention and the overall quality of the team and workplace.

Stay true
to yourself
*screw what
other people
think.*

DiSC profile

Created by the psychologist William Moulton Marston in the 1920s, the DiSC Profile assesses behavioural preferences based on four personality traits: Dominance (D), Influence (I), Steadiness (S), and Conscientiousness (C).

The DiSC Profile is widely used for personal and professional development, team building and leadership training.

Individuals benefit from the DiSC Profile by gaining insights into their communication preferences, work styles, and approaches to problem-solving. By understanding their behaviour and those of others, individuals can improve interpersonal relationships, resolve conflicts more effectively, and adapt their communication strategies to different situations. Organisations use the DiSC Profile to enhance team dynamics, improve employee engagement and create a more positive work culture based on mutual understanding.

The DiSC Profile is fantastic and I use it more often than not with everyone that I work with. Because of this I will only highlight further learning on this one.

The DiSC is extremely useful in understanding how someone naturally shows up and performs and how they have adapted to meet the needs of their role or the current workplace setup. The difference can speak volumes about what they need to be great in their role and how to find solutions to any issues that they may be having.

DiSC personality takeaways

- How you naturally perform / function
- How you have adapted to your environment
- Knowledge of what drives you
- Understanding of your strengths and weaknesses
- Realise what tends to overwhelm you and why
- Knowledge to support your mental health
- A toolkit for working with others well
- Understanding of how best to work with you for others
- Improved communications skills
- Clarity on why you struggle and at other times excel
- Viewpoint on the best type of work and roles for you

Understanding the value of authenticity and self-awareness are key steps to becoming the best version of yourself. Being authentic enables significant personal growth, while being fully aware of how you function and interact with others provides the foundation to move forwards in the best possible way for you.

How to get your sh!t sorted

Knowing who you are

- Understanding yourself creates authenticity enables accelerated personal growth and success.
- Being vulnerable and creating self-awareness are essential for balanced progress and resilience.
- Allowing for authentic self-expression leads to increased overall personal growth in life and work.
- Personality tests offer valuable insights into communication styles, strengths, and areas for development, enhancing personal and professional relationships.
- Recognising the power of authenticity and self-awareness plays a key part in becoming the best version of oneself.
- Authenticity empowers you to better face life's challenges with clarity and purpose.
- Ongoing self-exploration and reflection is fundamental to ongoing personal and professional development.

Digging deeper

Knowing who you are

- Reflecting on situations where I feel most authentic, how can I bring this authenticity into other aspects of my life or work?

- How does my level of self-awareness influence my relationships and interactions with others? What adjustments can I make to improve these?

- What daily practices or strategies can I create to bring about a greater self-awareness and authenticity in my actions and decisions?

- Are there specific fears or insecurities preventing me from fully being authentic and how can I deal with these?

- If I haven't already completed a personality test, would it be beneficial to take one now or revisit past results? How can I leverage this insight to align my actions with my authentic self and become the best version of myself?

Notes, musings and thoughts to myself

(Use these pages to make notes on what you've read to help get your sh!t together)

CHAPTER 8
Time management

CHAPTER 8
TIME MANAGEMENT

In this chapter, we explore the significance of time management for both personal and professional success. We highlight how the efficient use of time improves productivity and maintaining clarity on your goals. And that successful time management not only requires alignment with individual and professional objectives, but consistency and the use of the right tools to maintain focus and get the right things done. Binning that long to-do list and getting efficient and focussed!

I've done a lot of time management coaching with entrepreneurs and companies to help them become more productive, efficient, and clearer on what they should be working on that drives them forward. Within that time, I have developed ways of looking at time management that have helped myself and these individuals move forward successfully and cannot stress the importance of using your time in a smart way.

A fundamental part of your toolkit for the best version of you.

From my experience, the average person spends around 25% of their time thinking about taking action (or more realistically, thinking up excuses as to why they shouldn't take action) and the remainder of their time doing the immediate tasks in front of them.

Of the tasks being done, inefficient ways of working and poor time management mean that only a small fraction of this action moves them forward - and that's assuming that these actions are aligned to their goals / business strategy.

So often people ironically "don't have the time" to work on their time management or even know where to start. My advice would be you are better off taking your foot off the gas and working at 90% while 10% is spent reviewing how you can improve your time management and subsequent output and growth until you have that nailed. If you want to get ahead you need to be smart with your time.

or those who have no idea where to start, even the smallest changes will make a difference. A good starting point can be identifying what you could be doing better and establishing ways to stay on top of these so you can increase the amount of tasks that you are getting done - this often gives momentum to other improvements.

How are people generally doing?

- A shocking majority of **88% of individuals lack a dedicated time management system**, working instead without planning, as to-do lists or from email inboxes.

- **Only 12% (or one in eight people)** implement a specific time management system to organise themselves.

- 44% percent of people feel in control of their workload five days a week, while **46% experience a lack of control for one or two days weekly**, and 11% feel out of control for three or more days.

- Email habits vary, with **32% checking emails constantly**, 31% responding to notifications and 20% checking every hour.

- **The most popular time management technique is time blocking**, used by 5%, followed by Tony Robbins' RPM method (3%), and the Eisenhower Matrix (2%).

- Benefits of effective time management are widely recognised:
  91% report reduced stress at work
  90% see increased productivity
  86% enjoy improved work focus,
  82% gained more work confidence
  74% noted better collaboration with others.

Don't let yourself look back & realise how much time you wasted on dumb sh!t.

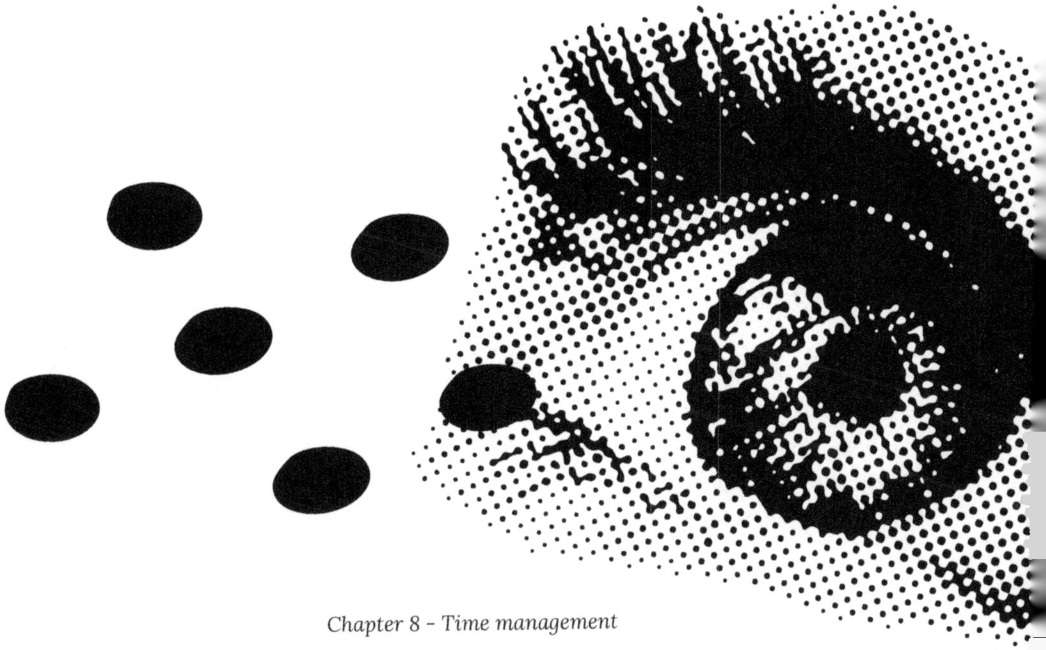

- A significant **76% would invest 15-30 minutes daily in time management if it meant saving 90 minutes**, reducing stress and enhancing work performance.

- Issues assessing the time work takes is common:
  38% of individuals spend up to an hour daily on irrelevant tasks or meetings
  32% waste 1-2 hours
  17% lose 2-3 hours on activities they shouldn't be spending time on

Procrastination as an excuse

There are a lot of posts online and POVs that pander to procrastination and the hints and tips to get things done. The Book Instantly Stop Procrastination by Patrick Dreschsier is dedicated to the topic. I myself have written a fair few posts on motivation and focus as opposed to procrastination.

However, my take on it is that some tasks are boring and quite frankly they make us want to poke our eyes out. But if you give a damn about moving forwards personally or with your business you need to just suck it up and get on with it. The more you do the more you want to do.

This creates the momentum that makes procrastination a thing of the past or at least not strong enough to stop you. So procrastination shouldn't be the focus, instead it is about being massively motivated and in tune with what we are doing that the work gets done regardless. All supported by the tools we use and the way we work which is specific to us.

Finding time

Another focus online when we look at time management is the amount of time we are able to find to do the work itself, from stories of early risers through to those who work on a continuous basis throughout weekends, and lest not forget those who have it nailed in a 4 hour day or even 4 day week now! With the right understanding of how you work, what you need to get done and tools that support you, you can find the time you need. As you will have heard before, we all have the same amount of time on a day to day basis to use.

But there is a lot more to time management than just getting things done and having time. Even the definition in the Oxford English dictionary term Time Management as: the ability to use one's time effectively or productively, especially at work.

I counter that true smart time management is not just about efficiency. One can be super efficient but if you are not happy in your career or out of depth in your work, efficiency will get things done but will it move you forward, and more importantly to where you want to be and fulfilled to boot? Surely without this level of depth one would never truly be motivated and as such the very reason you aren't getting things done? We cover the importance of the why and what later on in this book.

Consistency

So here this is again. While we may have covered some of this already, let's look at this in the context of time management. If you treat your time management like the average person treats eating well, then this will be inconsistent and demotivating when it goes wrong, actually counteracting the three weeks beforehand, for example, when you were managing your time well. Taking action on the things you need to do consistently requires effort.

Consistently delivering on what you need to do on a day-to-day basis is when the game changes. In the book "The Compound Effect" by Darren Hardy, he talks about the compound effect being the principle of reaping huge rewards from a series of small, smart choices consistently delivered on an ongoing basis. This is also highlighted in the book "The Slight Edge" by Jeff Olson.

These are very valuable ways to focus on improving what we do with our time, but in order to really make the most of your time to drive you forward, and in fact to be in the position to work less and achieve more, this requires us to go a little deeper.

Why time management matters

It makes sense that the more you are on top of your time the more you are moving forward and growing. If we are looking at time management from the angle of also ensuring that the time you spend is in line truly with what you should be spending both personally and career wise, then the benefits are:

- Increased focus
- Better quality output
- Less stress
- Increased growth (personal and business)
- More time
- Improved work life balance
- Reduced procrastination
- Productivity
- Improved fulfilment
- Alignment with purpose
- More earning potential
- Increased career opportunities

Time management matters because what you do creates the very world around you. How do all the most successful people in the world get to where they are? They are masters of their time and what to do with it and as such are continuously moving forward and growing. If you want to get ahead you need to be smart with your time and committed to that as a habit.

Getting things done

Once you have what you spend your time on aligned (we covered this in Chapter 6), it is now time to ensure that you will get things done, the HOW

To stay on top of tasks a high percentage of the population use to do lists or similar. While a list of tasks is useful, however it is missing two key components for actions on projects. The 'when' (when does it need to be completed by?) and also the 'how long' (how long will this task take me to complete?) If you were to randomly pick a task from your to-do list, how do you know that you will have enough time on that day to complete it and that it is being done in time without constantly doing this daily - the very obvious probability of failure will occur at some point.

Bin that to do list

The endless to do list. The list of tasks that gets worked on daily or weekly or monthly spending time moving and ticking off and adding to. The list that brings a sense of dread when you can see a whole bunch of things you should be doing. This ultimately is a massively inefficient way to stay on top of what you need to do. Here's why:

- Lack of strategic viewpoint
  With a list of tasks you don't know whether you are hitting what you need to do strategically and not getting swept into tasks that are wasting your time.

- Inefficient planning
  A long list of tasks means that you will spend a lot of time picking and choosing what you think you need to and adding new ones in. Wasting time on this daily adds up to a lot of time.

- Inability to prioritise
  A long list won't give you the opportunity to be able to prioritise easily and at a glance see what you need to do, in fact seeing a long list means that you may start on tasks that you feel are easier to do rather than the ones that are a real priority.

- Too much noise
  Looking at everything that you need to do daily is a big distraction and can have you thinking about all the different areas of the business which can distract your focus and slow you down. We can also have triggers that can distract us e.g. if an invoice needs paying and you can't do that yet, to remind yourself daily will only slow you down.

- **Feeling Overwhelmed**
  If you can see everything that you need to do in one hit, it is very easy to get overwhelmed and then not start a task or action at all. Why would we choose to see everything that we ultimately need to do each day and then expect ourselves to be motivated?

- **Missing the 'when' and 'how long'**
  So a list of tasks is useful, however in this form it is missing two key components for actions or projects as mentioned. The 'when', when do I need to complete this and when does it need to be completed by and also the 'how long'. How long will this task take me to complete? If you were to randomly pick a task from the list how do you know that you will have enough time on that day to complete it and that it is being done in time without constantly doing this daily with then the very obvious probability of failure at some point.

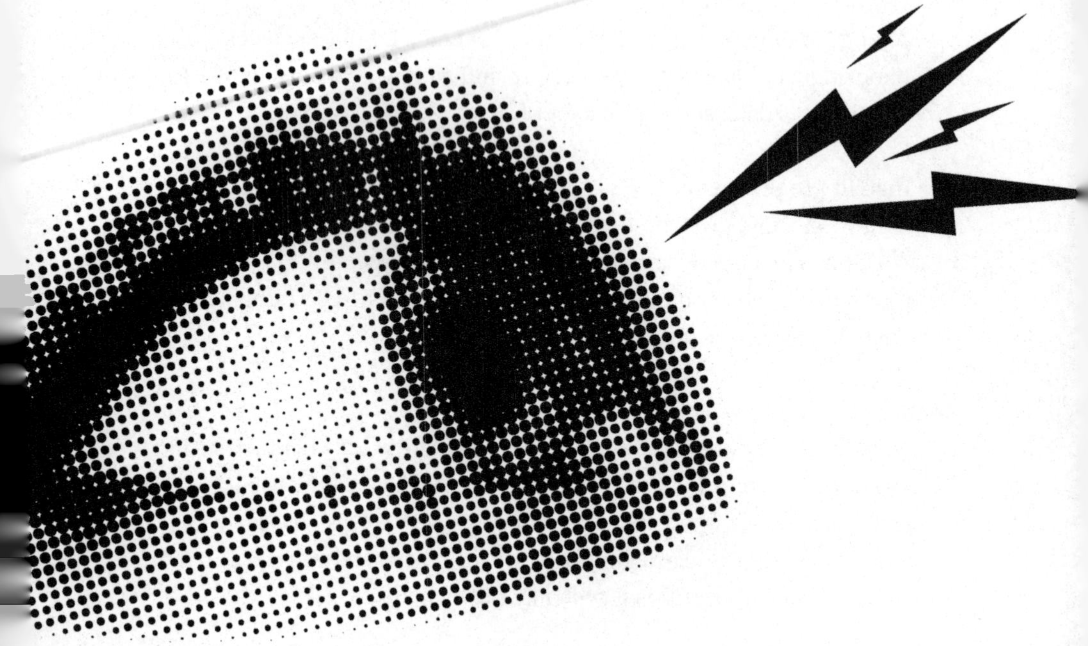

Getting Sh!t done

Ultimately, you need a way of working that helps you stay on top of what you need to do, and ensuring that what you are doing hits your targets, current strategy or even personal goals depending on what you are using your planning for that highlights the corresponding action you need to take that day are key. Then the rest is you sticking to that way of working, fine tuning where you need to and most importantly getting the tasks done!

Defining what it is you need to do

- Start from the top level with what you need to accomplish
- Breaking it down into sub projects or areas needed to achieve these
- Then smaller actions to achieve the outcomes for each of these
- Use a tool that helps you add in the 'when' and 'how long' or even 'who' where applicable
- Connect this to your diary or a feed through in to a list that you can see daily for what is due that day / week or month
- Review every few months

Getting tasks scheduled

Now you have noted what you need to do, using project management or task planning tools is a great way to centralise what you are working on and collaborate with others. Some great ones include Asana, Trello, or Monday, enabling you to add in those all-important tasks and timelines. You can also link these through to a daily task list or your diary. The key is to ensure that each day you can go to X point and know what you should be working on.

Tips for working smart

- Be clear on what you need to do
- Use tools that support how you work
- Action, action, action
- Build smart working into habits
- Develop routines
- Create accountability
- Know your working style
- Have a working schedule that suits you
- Assess output
- Review bi-yearly

What worked before may not work now, whether that be a role change or growth of you and your business, so a periodic review is always a good idea so you can adapt accordingly.

How to maintain it

- Don't overdo it and put yourself off
- Avoid measuring your time management against others routines
- Understand how long you can focus for and build it up
- Recognise when you are managing your time well
- Reward yourself, if you are too hard you won't maintain it
- Good time management is a habit, let it become one

As with any area, if you work on it you improve. Taking the time to fine tune how your time management is supporting you and your growth is pretty much one of the smartest things you can do with your time.

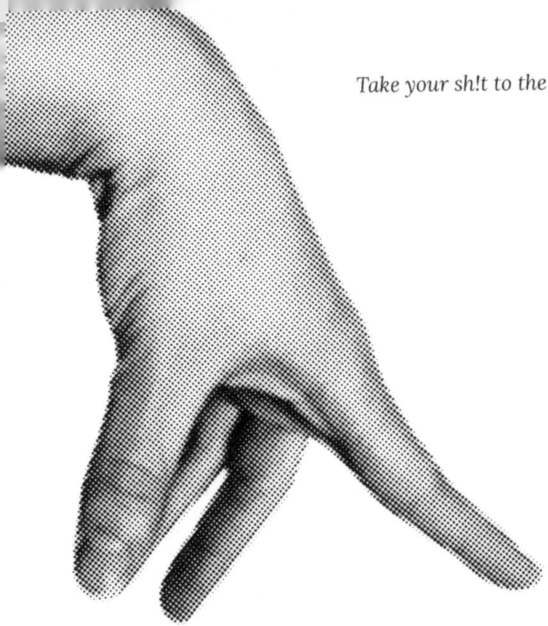

Stop
messing
about and
get on with it!

How to get your sh!t sorted

Time management

- Effective time management is key to achieving personal and professional goals with a clear focus on objectives.
- Be aware of the amount of time spent on immediate tasks versus strategic alignment and goal focussed actions.
- Even small adjustments in time management can result in huge improvements in productivity and overall momentum.
- Key challenges in time management include a lack of strategic foresight, inefficient planning and difficulty in prioritising tasks.
- Successful time management extends beyond mere efficiency, to the aligning actions with personal and professional objectives for growth.
- Consistency and adaptability are key for maintaining effective time management, requiring regular reviewing and adjusting.

Digging deeper

Time management

- Are my daily tasks directly contributing to my long-term goals and aspirations?
- If I am not using a time management tool already, could I use a tool like Asana, Trello, or Monday to streamline my workflow?
- Am I setting realistic deadlines and allocating sufficient time for each task, if not what needs to improve?
- What strategies can I bring in to minimise distractions and maintain focus while working?
- Are there any patterns of procrastination or wasting time in my day or week, what are these and how will I change this?
- Do I regularly review and adjust my time management strategies based on what I am getting done and what I am not getting around to?

Notes, musings and thoughts to myself

(Use these pages to make notes on what you've read to help get your sh!t together)

CHAPTER 9
Improving

CHAPTER 9
IMPROVING

This chapter presents some of my preferred tools and techniques, both personally used and observed in others that have been successfully used for ongoing improvement. With a focus on always striving to enhance and excel ensuring continuous growth. That alongside seeking ongoing improvement and learning from past mistakes makes this chapter a real value add.

We should be constantly looking to improve and be better at what we do. This ensures that we are on a constant path to growth. This has been a mantra to me for my whole life, always thinking of how to do something better and avoiding the same mistake twice.

So with this in mind, this chapter highlights some of my favourite tools and techniques either used by myself or others to ensure that you are improving. I've let rip here, so have fun!

Be *10%* better at everything *today*

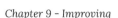

Stay sharp

You don't know what you don't know, you just can't see it. So to stay ahead you need to be constantly learning, from resources available, others and asking questions to expand your perception of where you are. Push yourself to discover new ideas or strategies or thinking. How can you expand your view of yourself, of others, your work or your industry? Surround yourself with super smart people who challenge you to be better and who you can learn from.

Peak performance mindset

If you are constantly hard on yourself or push to achieve anything of greatness, naturally our inner child will every now and again throw their toys out of the pram and counter what we are looking to do. And why can't life also be fun? To intentionally create moments of fun or rock and roll and really enjoy them, means that we will stay in the room when we need to maintain high performance in sustained periods. Or in fact anything for sustained periods. Allow for rock and roll.

Maintain your neuroplasticity to increase your ability to learn and grow. Dance, gaming, exercise and art all help to improve cognitive function and your capacity for growth. Keeping yourself sharp will mean that you are showing up on your A-game, spotting opportunities and spotting when you need to move or adapt or change. Learn to tap into feeling switched on and what that feels like. Bring this to your week not only in the work you do but in exercise, the more you do it the sharper you stay.

What can't you see?

Learn to tap into your best state as part of your toolkit to elicit and easily get into the zone when needed. What is your peak mindset? Sharp, focused and confident. Think of a time when you felt like that. How did you sit or stand, what did you feel like? Where were you and what did you see? Allow yourself to get back into the zone of how you felt. Do this often until you are able to switch into this zone on demand. Athletes/performers have it in their toolkit. So should you.

Allow for rock and roll

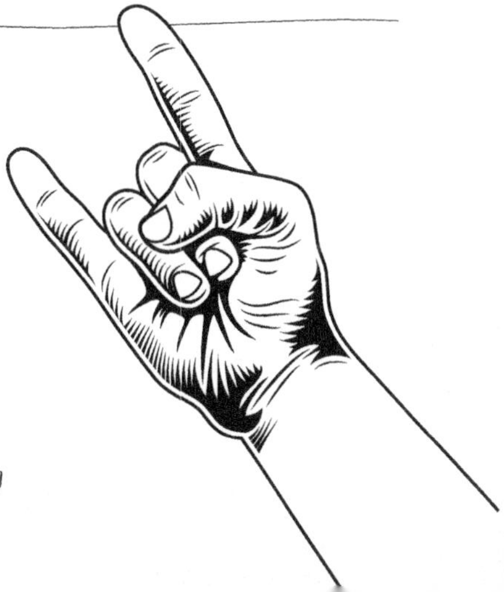

Don't worry about what others think

What if you decided to do everything 10% better. A tool that you can bring to the table twice a year to up your game substantially. What do I mean? Exactly as I said, be better or try harder by 10%, that bit more. Put that extra thought into what you are doing, saying, writing, who you are listening to, what you eat, how you dress, and how you show up. Everything. Sustain it for 1 month until you can see and feel the difference. The momentum you create for yourself from how great you feel, and the improved output makes this tool one for the long term.

Look after the **machine**

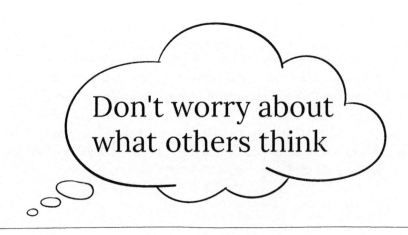

Be present. I mean really present. Stop thinking about what you need to do next or worrying about things. Being truly present at any given moment means that you will not only be your best, calm and centred and that you are able to read the room spotting opportunity for growth easily, have a better relationship with others, and connect with what you are actually doing on every level. Practise this for a day and see the difference in how you feel.

Worrying about what others are doing or questioning yourself slows you down. Just do what you need to do. The most successful entrepreneurs, did they worry about that? No. Exactly. Who gives a sh!t about what others think of you and what you are doing. For those that are able to master this, then you naturally create much more space, judgement-free to grow both professionally and personally.

Be 10% Better

Functioning at your optimum is eating the right food, getting enough sleep, and being fit. All the areas that I mentioned earlier in this book. No time? Not good enough, if you want to get ahead you need to be functioning at your best. Focus on the importance of functioning at this level has in achievement never mind with the increased ability to avoid burnout. If the average person is functioning at 50-70% of their natural ability based on this, think of what you could achieve? It is also important to keep well and making sure that the machine is functioning well will ensure this both now and in the future.

Notice the detail

Focus time

Know at any given point what you need to do. Got 2 hours? You should know exactly what it is that is of the most value to complete in that time and why. I cover this off in the time management section in terms of knowing what that is, however I am placing this here to stress the importance. I watched a recent interview with a well-known rapper and entrepreneur. He said that he always knew what he had done that day or week. He kept an awareness of the actions he was taking at any given moment. Know what yours should be to take your performance to that level.

Work with great people

Often at times we don't have the resources for what we are looking to achieve, either within us, practically or because people have told us or are telling us. What then happens is that we naturally limit our thinking with what we think is possible. What I've learned over the years is to just ignore this when deciding to do something and crack on regardless, even if I didn't want to. And how did I do that? By being brave and doing it anyway. Confidence and change follow an action, they don't start from nothing.

How long can you focus? Do you have a constant battle with finishing or getting engaged with tasks or projects? Figure this out what the time you are able to focus on is to avoid battles with yourself. Spend a few days noticing when you tend to struggle and the time you focus for. Then work in sprints matching your focus time with 5-10 min breaks in between for increased productivity and output.

Know what **you** need to do

The people you work with are an extension of what you are able to do. Therefore, make sure that you surround yourself with great people who can really extend what you are able to achieve but that you also enjoy working with. These two areas combine to create awesome momentum around your achievement as a team, group, or friends. And the benefit is that you will also maintain a high level of output.

Being **brave**

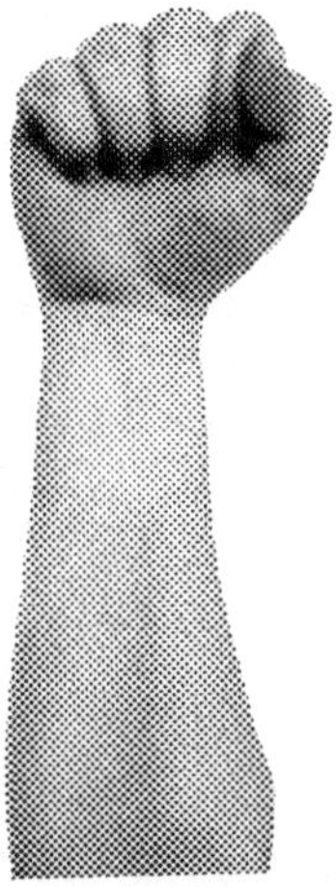

Face your *fear*

Make decisions and stop messing about. If you want to plough through what you need to do, it involves maintaining a strong level of decisiveness and decision-making flow. Day to day, the average person wastes a hell of a lot of time dithering about between this point. Just get on with it. Now, I am not suggesting you make rushed, foolhardy decisions but ultimately if you decide to be more decisive then the percentage of movement forwards increases.

Five things rule

12345

Use the latest in AI tools to work smart and reduce wasted time on tasks that you could get done much faster. It is so important to start to implement and use AI in your day-to-day life individually and within the workplace or your business. In a few years' time, if not essentially, it will be like you running alongside a car to try to keep up. Get involved.

You learn the most about yourself and experience the most growth when you face your fear. We are so used to looking for achievement or growth from the areas we can build on and that are 'positive' so to speak. But how about turning achievement on its head and facing the things that we REALLY don't want to. If we fear or avoid something it creates a barrier to what we can achieve and who we can become. Remove this barrier and watch yourself rise.

Be *decisive*

Struggling to get things done? Less is more. Often we can pick so many items to do that we only get a small amount done in the end, making us feel defeated even though we got the tasks we did on our desk that day. Instead, proactively pick 5 things each day to complete that add value to where you are looking to get to. Feeling like you are achieving, you will then naturally do more. Avoid the procrastination trap and allow yourself to feel like you are achieving to actually do more.

AI *tools*

(Artificial intelligence)

Get rid of *time wasters*

Don't accept breadcrumbing. People drip-feeding you conversations around potentially needing something or vice versa. Have a 3-meeting rule before you then put cards on the table, pull back, and move on. Also, decide whether someone needs your time at all. Be mindful of how much free time you give others and the value exchange there for you. To really ensure that you are improving, you need to create the space to spend time with those that will help you get there.

Death ground

Functioning at the level where you will perform at your highest is ideal. Death ground is a military term where soldiers are put into the mindset that there is no retreat, fight or die. Creating an elevated sense of urgency and desperation which substantially boosts their performance. Simply put, they are on death ground and fighting for their lives. By reducing timelines and creating a sense of urgency, you are intentionally eliciting the thinking needed to drive forwards at this exceptional level. Just like exam cramming, when we have to, it gets done.

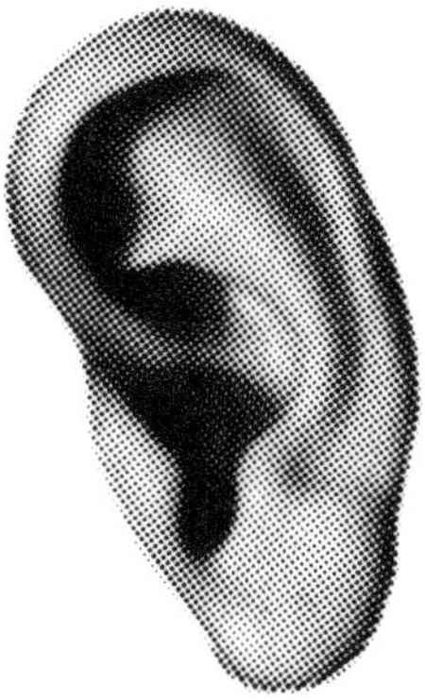

Work on your life **when things are going *well*.**

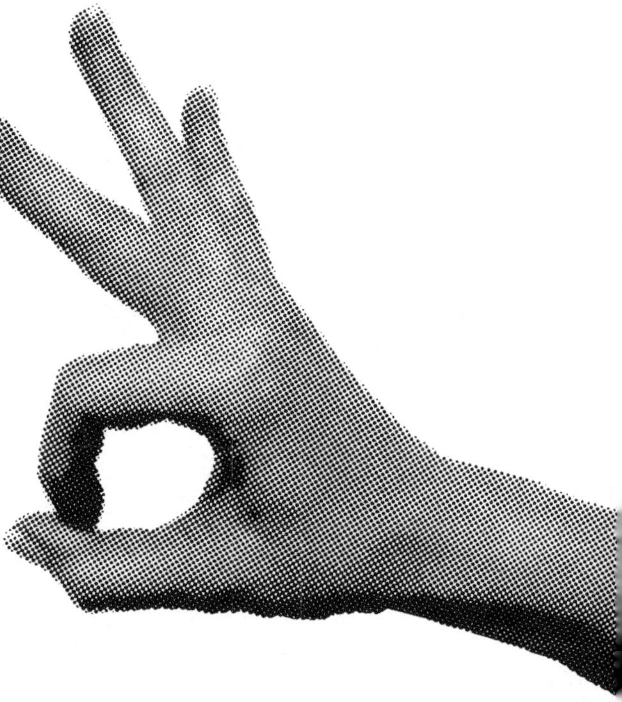

How to get your sh!t sorted

Improving

- **Develop your own toolkit** of strategies that help you constantly improve
- **Stay sharp** - maintain mental agility
- **What you can't see** - embrace ongoing learning
- **Peak performance mindset** – be able to tap into your best mental state
- **Allow for rock and roll** – let go to balance out hard work
- **Don't worry about what others think** - embrace authenticity
- **Be 10% better** - strive for continuous improvement
- **Look after the machine** – look after yourself
- **Notice the detail** - practise mindfulness and awareness
- **Focus time** - improve productivity through focused periods
- **Being brave** - embrace challenges for growth
- **Work with great people** - create excellence through collaboration
- **Know what you need to do** - prioritise tasks effectively
- **Face your fear** - confront challenges for personal growth

Notes, musings and thoughts to myself

(Use these pages to make notes on what you've read to help get your sh!t together)

CHAPTER 10
Measuring results

CHAPTER 10

MEASURING RESULTS

In this final chapter, we look into reviewing and measuring progress. We explore areas for improvement through practical insights and exercises. This chapter provides tools for measuring different areas discussed in the book and for future use, for continued personal growth towards becoming the best version of yourself.

So you've completed the book, great stuff. Now here you will find several tools and ways of measuring the results to ensure that you are making the continuous movement forwards to becoming the best version of yourself. Given that we should always be working on ourselves and who we are, they have been designed in such a way that you can use these exercises again and again to measure, review and improve.

Know when to let go and move on

The best version of you: staying on track

- Area
  Down on the left of the page, you have "Area," which highlights each of the aspects for the best version of yourself.

- Current
  This indicates your current situation on a scale of 1-5, with 1 indicating low or 'poor performance' and 5 indicating 'high'.

- What great looks like
  This defines where you would like to be in terms of score and what that would entail. For example, under "Physical," it could be a low score currently. In "What great looks like," you would put, for instance, a 3, aiming for mid-level fitness with "How" being cycling twice a week for 30 minutes.

- Timelines
  Add in the current date and the date you are looking to achieve the improved output by.

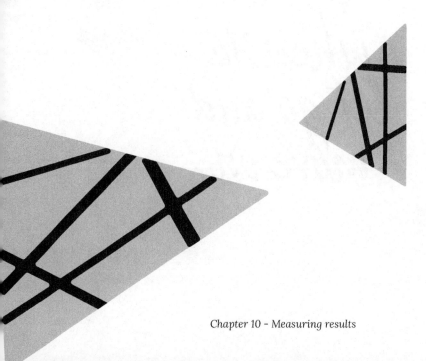

Date:

Area	**Current (1-5)**	**What great looks like**	**(1-5)**	**How?**	**Date achieved**
Physical					
Mindset					
Energy					
Habits					
Action					
Knowing yourself					
Time management					

The best version of you: asking the right questions

Here are key questions to ask yourself that will help you to create the right type of thinking and awareness of your journey towards becoming the best version of you.

Daily Questions

- Did I make the right type of progress towards my goals today?
- Did I act with kindness and empathy towards others?
- Did I learn something new today?
- Did I take care of my physical and mental health today?
- Did I manage my time effectively and focus on actions that move me forwards?
- Did I maintain a positive attitude and mindset throughout the day?
- Did I practise gratitude and appreciation for what I have?
- Did I challenge myself to step out of my comfort zone?

Weekly Questions

- Did I achieve the milestones I set for myself this week?
- Did I invest time in meaningful relationships and connections?
- Did I take steps to improve my skills and knowledge?
- Did I handle challenges and setbacks with resilience and adaptability?
- Did I maintain a healthy work-life balance?
- Did I contribute positively to my community or environment?
- Did I reflect on my progress and areas for improvement?
- Did I celebrate my accomplishments and successes?

Monthly Questions

- Did I make significant progress towards my long-term goals this month?
- Did I demonstrate consistent growth and improvement in various areas of my life?
- Did I identify and address any recurring challenges or obstacles?
- Did I invest time in self-care and personal development activities?
- Did I build on important relationships and express gratitude to those around me?
- Did I maintain a sense of purpose and alignment with my values?
- Did I seek feedback and constructive criticism to fuel my growth?
- Did I set new goals and focus for the upcoming month based on my reflections?

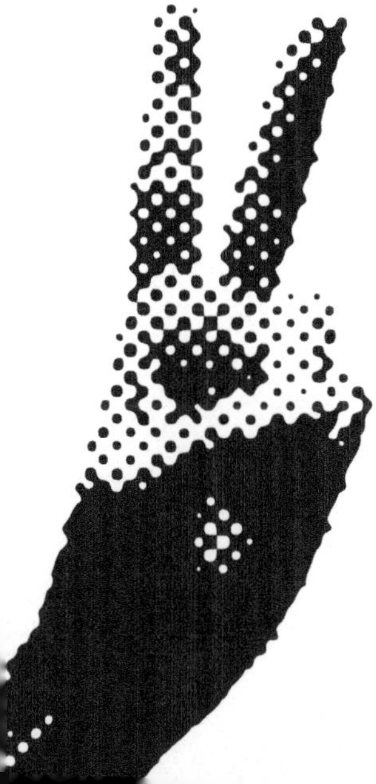

Key Question (*for all questions*):
What do I need to do in order to improve or maintain these?

The best version of you: % of time exercise

This is hands down one of my favourite exercises. I have done this myself with other individuals, and with teams in multi-million-pound companies.

This exercise will help you see where you are currently spending your time, how much of it, where it should be spent ideally and what that time looks like. Finally, it identifies the actions you need to take to help you get there.
The exercise of doing this in the first place is such an eye-opener to where you spend your time. Here are some examples of how this tool can be used:

How you spend your time:

- Individually (personal)
- In your role or business (work)
- With others or teams you collaborate with (those around you)

It can also be used when needing clarity in a particular area. For example, if you are struggling to see the details behind why you still have so many emails, then do a percentage of time split breaking down your management of those and what they are and where they are coming from to give you clarity about how to improve this.

This can also be used to see where your team is spending time or your colleagues to bring about transparency and removal of workflow bottlenecks. Do note that sometimes it may take you a while to complete the details for the areas as we don't always reflect in this way, but that is a good thing!

I would recommend doing this exercise at least twice a year for yourself in your personal life and the same for your work. You can also see the shared learning from both of these together. Interestingly, when this is done, some of the actions to improve areas cross over from business to personal and vice versa.

Area	Current %	Goal %	Actions to improve

How to get your sh!t sorted

Measuring results

- How can I effectively apply the measurement tools provided to assess my progress and areas for improvement?
- What specific actions can I take based on the insights gained from reviewing my time management and areas for growth?
- How will I set clear and achievable goals that align with the measurements and insights obtained?
- What strategies will I implement to track my progress over time and hold myself accountable for achieving my goals?
- How can I seamlessly integrate these measurement tools into my daily routine to enable continuous personal development?
- Are there additional resources or support networks I can use to enhance my measurement and review process?
- How will I celebrate my successes along the way to keep me engaged and motivated?
- How will I commit to using the measurement and review tools provided in this book to ensure sustained progress on my journey towards becoming the best version of myself?

Notes, musings and thoughts to myself

(Use these pages to make notes on what you've read to help get your sh!t together)

Congratulations

YOU'VE

TAKEN YOUR

SH!T

TO THE NEXT LEVEL

Printed in Great Britain
by Amazon

42087723R00106